Praise for "Going Home"

"Most pain in peoples' lives come down to self-defeating behaviors and this book is the prescription for healing physically, emotionally and spiritually. Drs.. Greg and Lori Boothroyd have combined their talents in a book that touches and teaches at the same time. This book is a combination of experienced clinical techniques, common sense, humor and motivation for improving our lives. I congratulate them on their abilities to help those who have wandered from a path inflicted with self pain by sharing the map, benchmarks and techniques for "Going Home".

- Robert J. Ackerman, Ph.D.
Professor of Sociology
Indiana University of Pennsylvania
Author, Perfect Daughters, Silent Sons and Chicken Soup for the Recovering Soul

"This book offers a clear, accessible, and useful roadmap for finding ourselves when we feel stuck and lost in the rocky terrain of life. The authors weave together solid principles of traditional and positive psychology, and apply these theories to both the individual and to the larger world of relationships and organizations. Better yet, these ideas are interwoven with extraordinary warmth and wit, and a recognition that the journey toward healing is well served by having compassion for ourselves. This mixture of ingredients brings heart and soul to *Going Home*, and makes it a delight to read."

- Karen Horneffer, PhD, Director, Holistic Health Care Program, Western Michigan University, Assistant Professor, Licensed Psychologist

"This gem of a book is the ultimate in recognizing life's challenges and the painful grief of self defeating behaviors. Drs.. Gregory and Lori Boothroyd use their exquisite humor, gentleness and exceptional knowledge in a design that is simplicity and encouragement personified. Common sense is the keynote. None of this unintelligible psycho-babble. It is real, helpful and at times very witty. Dr. Gregory is unique in his approach, his kindness and laughter......................and then there is Lori. I have used the Psychic Garden in presentations since reading the book - utter magic. Having been involved in the field of People Work since 1951 and Thanatology since 1974, I have read thousands of books - this is among the very best."

- Reverend Dr. Yvonne Kaye, International Speaker, Thantalogist, Author, Columnist and Laughter Addict.
North Wales, Pennsylvania.

"Drs. Lori and Greg Boothroyd share their successful approach to treating self-defeating behaviors in a manner that is uncomplicated, easy to read, sensible and free of psycho-babble. With warmth and wit, the reading is both light and delightful while at the same time clinically insightful and comprehensive in depth of the subject matter. A great guide for those of us who have lost our way."

-Timothy J. Allen, M.A.
Executive Director, Assessment and Treatment Services Center, Newport Beach, CA

"Since its first publication, my clients have found *Going Home* to be a clear, readable and inspirational roadmap for replacing their self-defeating behaviors with life-giving ones. This latest edition includes a fresh, new section which provides ideas and direction for implementing the book's theories and strategies. Well done, Greg and Lori!"

- Sara Sue Schaeffer, Ed.D., LPC, LMFT. Past Chair, Michigan Board of Counseling. Past President, Michigan Counseling Association.

"Greg and Lori have upgraded and sharpened the focus of *Going Home*. The clarity of their contrasting self-defeating and life-giving behaviors results in positive new directions as we confront life problems and work to grow within ourselves. As a problem-solving guide, this is a must for those caught in the web of their own self-destructiveness."

- Donald A. Amidon, D.Min., LPC, LMFT, MAC. Former Chief, Chaplain Service, Veteran's Affairs Medical Center, Battle Creek, MI.

"I have always appreciated any clinical approach that is utilitarian. *Going Home: A Positive Emotional Guide for Promoting Life-Generating Behaviors* takes such a handy and practical approach. Dramatically opposed to the adage "too stupid to get out of one's own way" - an all to often edict found in clinical manuals where the therapist tells the client exactly what to do - Dr's. Boothroyd provide a map with instructions that say "you already have what you need, just get out of your own way and let it happen". By letting the healing part inside take over, a positive psychology full of strength and hope - not fear - can get you what you need. It has been a pleasure to read the Boothroyd's book. I think they are right. A little humor, a good map and some personal effort can get one a long way in this world. Check this book out, but do it with caution. You might actually find yourself changing for the better!"

- Cardwell C. Nuckols MA, PhD
Dr. Nuckols has been described as "one of the most influential clinical trainers in America." His passion and mission is to assist in the translation of emerging scientific research into information and techniques helpful to those who do the important work of helping alcoholics, addicts and those suffering from co-occurring disorders find their personal road to recovery.

Going Home

A Positive Emotional Guide for Promoting Life-Generating Behaviors

Gregory W. Boothroyd, Ph.D., CAC II, L.P.C
Lori A. Gray Boothroyd, Ph.D., L.L.P.

honu
PUBLICATIONS

ISBN: 0-9671416-1-3

Honu Publications (formerly Greenwood Associates)
P.O. Box 601
Traverse City, MI 49685

Printed in the United States of America.

This publication is designed to provide authoritative information in regard to the subject matter covered. It is sold with the understanding that the publisher is not engaged in rendering psychological, medical, or other professional services. This book is not intended to replace the services of a competent professional, in the event that counseling or psychological intervention is needed.

AUTOBIOGRAPHY
IN FIVE SHORT CHAPTERS

By Portia Nelson

Chapter One

I walk down the street.
There is a deep hole in the sidewalk.
I fall in.
I am lost.....I am helpless.
It isn't my fault.
It takes forever to find a way out.

Chapter Two

I walk down the same street.
There is a deep hole in the sidewalk.
I pretend I don't see it.
I fall in again.
I can't believe I'm in the same place; but it isn't my fault.
It still takes a long time to get out.

Chapter Three

I walk down the same street.
There is a deep hole in the sidewalk.
I see it is there.
I still fall in.....it's a habit.
My eyes are open.
I know where I am.
It is my fault.
I get out immediately.

Chapter Four

I walk down the same street.
There is a deep hole in the sidewalk.
I walk around it.

Chapter Five

I walk down another street.

DEDICATIONS

To my granddaughters Sonna and Leighton Boothroyd and the
roadmaps they so effortlessly provide toward
Going Home.

To Scott & Jeff, and Dianna & Jana Boothroyd, once sons and
daughter-in-laws...now good friends.

To Mark, Perry, Pete and Phil Boothroyd.......
my big brothers.

And

To my loving wife Lori...more than a partner, more than a friend,
more than a miracle.

GB

To the dear children in my life, Andrew and Katie Gray.

To the memory of my Grandmother, Aleen R. Tarrant, whose
Heart was always my Home.

And to my husband Gregory: I am eternally grateful to you for
holding my heart in your hands.

LGB

ACKNOWLEDGMENTS

I am deeply grateful to my friends Dr. Robert Ackerman, Tim Allen, Dr. Edward Gondolf and Dr. Yvonne Kaye for prompting, encouraging and supporting this book.

I'm indebted to my students and my clients who helped me help them find their rightful path toward goin' home.

Special thanks to Dan Barmettler, his staff, and the wonderful participants he continues to draw in the Institute for Integral Development training conferences.

And always to Milt Cudney..............thanks.

GB

I am forever indebted to my parents, Gary and Diane Gray, who continue to encourage me to use my gifts and to never give up. I am so very grateful to have a friend who has made me laugh and never ceased to encourage me through the years - Rachael Schmidt. My love to each of you.

My advisors, mentors and friends who helped me on my professional paths: Drs. Lois Alexander, Molly Vass, Nancy Crewe and Karyn Boatwright. Thank you for lighting the way for me.

Finally, I'm thankful to my students and clients who have taught and guided me along the way.

LGB

CONTENTS

OVERVIEW

After many years of service as counselors, instructors and consultants to education, industry and government, we have never met anyone who at some point or another in their life didn't practice self-defeating behaviors or attitudes. It seems to be an unintentional yet predictable consequence from growing up in our families and our culture. While such behaviors begin unwittingly, through years of practice they eventually become unwieldy and box in the best we have to offer ourselves and our world.

Self-defeating behaviors take many forms – the most common of which include:

Low Self-Concept
Underachievement
Substance Abuse
Indecision
Excessive Worry
Perfectionism
Pessimistic Thinking
Depressive Tendencies
Lack of Energy
Defensiveness
Dependency
Procrastination
Alienation
Disorganization
Holistic Depletion
Irresponsibility
Self-criticism
Excessive Introspection
Apathy
Overeating

These behaviors are defeating because they interfere with our health, joy, productivity, relationships, spiritual and emotional growth and serenity. They prevent us from "generating life" from within and enjoying our life to its fullest capability.

It is important to note that behaviors take place on a *continuum,* ranging from "typical" to "pathological". For example, all of us worry at times or feel fatigue, but when these behaviors take place to such a degree that they override or shadow our strengths and skills, they then become self-defeating. It is also important to note that conditions such as severe clinical depression, which reside at the far end of continuum, are best served by the intervention of mental health professionals. Most of us practice at least a few behaviors which lie somewhere near the middle of this continuum – troubling and self-defeating, but not necessarily "diagnosable". This book provides tools for working with troubling behaviors that interfere with life generating behaviors – those behaviors that allow our strengths to shine and our enjoyment of life to flourish.

Just as individuals practice self-defeating behaviors, so too do couples, families, departments, organizations, corporations, school systems, and nations. These relational and systemic defeating behaviors take many forms including:

Impaired Communication
Reluctance to Compromise
Little to No Cooperation
Lack of Intimacy
Power Struggles
Group Disorganization
Lack of Teamwork
Group Incompetence
Little or No Innovation
Group Impotence
Competing Divisions or Departments
Gridlock

The exhaust from such systemic and relational defeating behaviors predictably yields boredom, cynicism, group/familial dissension, low production, low morale and high employee truancy and turnover. Specifically in spousal/ domestic partner relationships, self-defeating behaviors lead to draining, lonely, impaired relationships, often followed by divorce or termination of partnership.

Traditional therapeutic efforts to resolve typical individual, relational and systemic defeating behavior patterns have too frequently been unsuccessful because they tend to overvalue the exploration of the past and the *why* of unhealthy behavior. Psychotherapists, by nature of traditional training, are also often not equipped to provide simple, useful tools for promoting positive change in their clients. Lack of success has also resulted from our incessant need as therapists to believe that replacing self-defeating behaviors with life-generating behaviors is necessarily a complicated, lengthy and mysterious process. From our collective experience over the years, nothing could be further from the truth. All that's essentially required is a compass and a map to help us get out of our own way and honor the healthy choices and attitudes that already lie within us – waiting to capitalize on their wisdom.

This book is designed as a guide and roadmap to find and use those choices that lead to life generating behavior. It's divided into four sections. The first section, "Leaving Home" attempts to briefly explain and demystify the origin of our self-defeating behaviors. Section two, "Wandering and Getting Lost," reveals the insanity, folly and pain associated with continuing these behaviors long after they've betrayed us. The third section, "Going Home," lays out a clear concise 12-step roadmap to rediscover and recapture the direction we need to get on with our emotional growth and spiritual journey. The final section, "Assessment and Application" provides suggestions for the further nurturing of life generating behavior through"Psychic Gardening" and suggests future directions for applying the theory.

Unlike so many altogether too serious self-help books, "Going Home" attempts to remain light, warm, personal and instructional. It's also relatively brief and uncomplicated in order to remove mystery from the inner growth process. Hence, it should appeal to any person, couple, family or system wishing to rediscover joy, purpose, meaning and serenity. It is also obviously appropriate for professionals and students in areas such as counseling, psychology, social work, professional coaching, health promotion, human resources, or substance abuse treatment.

This new edition of "Going Home" incorporates updated and expanded information, including a deeper inspection of relational and systemic defeating behaviors and more specific applications of the theory (e.g. substance abuse treatment). A companion exercise called "Psychic Gardening," is a supplemental self-assessment tool intended to assist in the identification of strengths and the ingredients necessary to grow life generating behaviors. The theory is also framed within the emerging, dynamic field of Positive Psychology, which is the first psychological science of human strengths.

Also included in this edition are highlighted "voices" of individuals who have utilized the theory's principles in their lives and shared their personal experiences and triumphs. We share them with you as means of illustrating the concepts and giving them life. The people, events and experiences described in these captions are true and accurate; however, names and identifying details have been altered to protect privacy.

Finally, this new edition introduces the co-author, Lori Gray Boothroyd. Author initials after major headings will guide you as the informal and personal voices of the authors alternate and intermingle throughout the book.

PREFACE

GB:

I've always stayed clear of reading self-help books. While I collect them, particularly those written by good friends or acquaintances, I never seem to read them. They're on my bookshelves, coffee tables, toilet-tank tops and office desks where they can be noticed—especially the ones with personal inscriptions to me by the author. I display them like conversation pieces and, when they're acknowledged by my guests, I use the opportunity to talk at length about the author and the book as if I had read it or written it myself.

The origin of my resistance to reading this stuff is hard for me to isolate. Part of it, I suppose, has to do with a natural tendency since I was a kid to be active and doing things instead of sitting and reading. But even when I was forced to read during my doctoral program, I did the least I could and always with immense yet quiet resistance. During my oral exam when I was defending my dissertation, a committee member suggested that I "go back to the library" to get additional supporting data to bolster some conclusions I had made in the final chapter. When I spontaneously responded "Where's the library?" everyone on the committee laughed at what they thought was a joke. It wasn't! I had no idea where the library was located. Quickly recognizing that my remark was dangerously funny, I bought a campus map, found the library, got my work done, graduated, and got out of there.

I suspect another part of my reluctance to read self-help books and professional literature has to do with a long career of being a therapist. It can be grueling work and I have personally witnessed the professional burnout of many friends and colleagues, particularly in the area of chemical dependency treatment where client resistance is especially strong. Somehow, after thousands of hours of client-therapist conversations, the idea of spending my free time with a book on the same subject simply didn't measure up to a good one on mountain climbing or kayaking.

Having acknowledged this attitude and disposition, it was both surprising and somewhat amusing that I ever created this self-help book to begin with. While the motivation to write remains unclear, it seems to have primarily been driven by requests and encouragement from friends and clients as well as a developing desire from within to share personal and professional ideas, memories and stories that have added meaning to my life. The original edition of this book was clearly prompted by Dr. Robert Ackerman, one of my oldest and dearest friends whose array of successful books make up many of my conversation pieces. During dinner in St. Louis, Missouri, following a workshop he invited me to present, Bob used six restaurant napkins to outline his version of the book I should author.

Serious additional encouragement to write came from my 24 year association with Dr. Milton Cudney who was my teacher, friend, colleague, co-trainer, co-workshop leader and confidant. During the years prior to his death, he repeatedly urged me to write and share my own personal understanding, application and refinement of the theory he created on Eliminating Self-Defeating Behaviors. "You've got a book growing in you," he'd say, "and you gotta give it life."

Certainly another influence on the original undertaking evolved from my national workshop audiences as well as graduate students in my lectures combining self-defeating behavior theory and substance abuse treatment. The common denominator of their collective feedback was a directive to write a book in the same personal, humorous, straight-forward and uncomplicated manner that I use while teaching and presenting programs.

Following such generous encouragement, the book was launched with the singular intent that it be used as a supplement to my workshops and courses and available for whomever wished to deepen their understanding and application of the material. During that first printing, I had no idea that the book would rather soon come to be read and enjoyed independent of classes and conferences as a free-standing source of direction toward personal growth. Therapists and agencies from around the country began ordering copies for their clients. Teachers and professors did the same for their students. A second printing became necessary; then a third along with the development of the website www.drboothroyd.com.

I, along with future readers, am fortunate in that the need for a fourth printing came at a time when my wife Lori was willing to thoughtfully revise and expand the content of the book. As a gifted psychologist, college teacher and professional coach, she brings to this revised edition a much needed bridge to contemporary theories of change and human strengths.

Her contributions, coupled with expanded thought on defeating systems and substance abuse application, are designed to further assist all of us in increasing life-generating behavior. Together, we hope this book sheds light on how and why we abandon our psychic and spiritual homes and what we can do to rediscover and recover our rightful path toward Going Home.

LGB:

I too am a collector of many self-help books, but unlike my husband, I have actually read many of them. Probably too many! By the time I'd entered a doctoral program in counseling psychology, I had already tried on so many theoretical "hats" and approaches to self-improvement that I grew intensely discouraged and confused. When I suggested to my doctoral committee members that I was interested in pursuing ways of making meaning from life experiences as well as promoting quality of life in myself and my clients, I was further discouraged to see blank (if not slightly bemused) stares in response to my hopeful mission statement. It wasn't pretty. For the next few years I learned about assessment and diagnosing clinical psychopathology, but felt a quiet indignation and a certainty that I and the field were missing the big picture, or perhaps looking at the 'picture' of mental health through a limiting black and white lens, versus a full spectrum of color. Why were we focusing only on weakness and pathology in our clients? What about the role of individual strengths, positive characteristics, or spirituality? Why aren't we helping people learn how to live happier, meaningful lives? I was asking these questions to a room full of people who were known to perform a 'happy dance' after "successfully" diagnosing the latest pathology from the DSM-IV (the bible of psychopathology). I wasn't knocking the importance of professional diagnostic skills, yet this very emphasis seemed to dis-empower my clients and often didn't inform or support the therapeutic process. I felt like a despairingly odd duck in the pond. Little did I know then that hope was on the way – literally.

In the year 2000, an issue of a professional journal was published which focused on an emerging field called Positive Psychology. Normally turned off and somewhat bored by the professional journals, I instead almost drooled with excitement as I absorbed the pages! Here was a new science of human strengths which emphasized learning more about what is positive and healthy in the human condition. What I found was theoretical footing and a place from which to launch my otherwise eccentric and boorish tirade of frustrations and complaints about the field of psychology and counseling. Subsequent research and my doctoral dissertation focused on a theory of hopeful thinking as I began to make meaning within my educational and training experiences. This was a major stepping stone and a professional turning point, not to mention that I no longer felt I had imprisoned myself through my vocational choices.

The second stepping stone occurred as I was completing my clinical training at Western Michigan University, when I was introduced to the self-defeating behavior theory from my colleague, Dr. Gregory Boothroyd. This was a theory that assumed we are healthy, whole individuals who sometimes lose our way, but can find our way back to optimal quality of life by "Going Home". This was a theory that successfully integrated numerous theoretical viewpoints and didn't conflict with corresponding interventions; it could be applied in conjunction with other treatments for serious pathology. It could be used alone as primary or secondary prevention and psychoeducation. This was a theory that could easily be taught to individuals to help themselves and others; you didn't have to have a doctorate to reap benefits. In short, this was a theory that took the babble out of psychobabble!

I can assure you I am not a lonely cheerleader; nor am I biased because I married the man who taught me the theory. Greg and I receive letters and emails from all over the country and parts of the world sharing with us stories of personal and professional successes. I have sat in audiences and classrooms to observe the positive reactions and responses from workshop participants. More recently, I have taught the theory to my own students at a private liberal arts college where beyond the classroom I still hear stories of continued growth that these bright students experience through their application of the theory. Happily, I have integrated this theory into my work as a psychologist and it is a great tool in my psychotherapy "toolbox".

The other exciting application I am now experiencing is in my work as a professional psychological coach. This kind of coaching has nothing to do with blowing a whistle or doing pushups! The purpose of professional coaching is to work as a partner to develop and implement strategies that will help clients reach personally identified goals of enhanced performance and personal satisfaction. Coaching can address a wide variety of goals including specific personal projects, life balance, job performance and satisfaction as well as more general conditions in personal lives, businesses, or professions. As you will see later in the book, the theory is an ideal tool for professional coaches. For more detailed information about coaching, visit my website www.lifeexpansion.com.

All of these new ideas and application additions prompted Greg and I to revise and create a co-authored edition of this book. I can only hope that my contributions and voice enhance what is already a loved and well-received book.

We both hope you find it enjoyable and useful.

INTRODUCTION

**"Goin' home, goin' home, I'm jes' goin' home;
It's not far, jes' close by, Through an open door.
I'm jes' goin' home."**

GB:
As a graduation present following completion of elementary school, I bought myself a ukulele. It came with an instruction booklet of basic chords and a number of beginner's songs like "O' Susannah," "Jingle Bells," "Goin' Home," "Old Man River," and others which I quickly mastered. While most of the songs got stored in my memory and left for retrieval around the campfires and Christmases of my life, "Goin' Home" lingered. It simply wouldn't go away. It was forever ready to be hummed, whistled, played and sung—often times with me breaking into tears before I could finish. I'm sure the people who heard me sing it were baffled at the babbling, sobbing mess I'd render myself. While I couldn't explain the intensity of my feelings, I somehow knew that this particular music served as a key to unlocking my heart and the path to joy, reverence and serenity. Simply put, "Goin' Home" hit home and it's done so ever since.

Some years later, after indulging anyone who'd listen to my developing ukulele talents, I decided with the help of my parents to include classical music in my diet of life-generating foods. I can recall almost falling over in disbelief upon first hearing a recording of Anton Dvorak's Symphony No. 9 in E minor, Op. 95 "From the New World." There in the second movement "Largo" was my favorite ukulele hit tune "Goin' Home" which Dvorak had composed in 1893. Inspired by Longfellow's epic, The Song of Hiawatha, "Largo" recalls the funeral of Minnehaha.

I knew nothing about Longfellow, Hiawatha, Minnehaha or William Fisher who wrote the lyrics to "Goin' Home" seventy-five years later. What I do know is that I promptly put my uke away and proceeded to wear that record out. It's been replaced many times and I now have it in the durable form of a compact disc. Through all the years, this music has continued to speak to me—reminding me each time that within all of us is a deep, rich, spiritual soil from which the best of life grows and connects us, giving us opportunity to grow and flourish.

So, what's all this got to do with the eliminating of self-defeating behaviors and the subsequent promotion of life-generating behaviors? Well, the answer is that I don't really know. It just feels like it does. Each time I witness a client or student come up from their own particular bottom by getting rid of defeating behavior patterns and getting reattached to their very best spiritual and psychic self, "Goin' Home" plays again in my heart. Hunger for home through the rediscovery and recovery of joy, purpose and serenity seems to be a collective symptom. Why and how these life-affirming needs get abandoned from the soil banks of our lives in the first place will be shared in Part I, Leaving Home.

Leaving Home

The Story of Stephanie
Author Unknown

A man came home from work one night with his briefcase jammed full of work that his boss insisted be completed by the next morning. It was a lot of work! As he walked in the door of his home, his wife greeted him with a kiss, helped him with his coat and then put on her coat and kissed him good-bye. When he asked her where she was going she reminded him, as she had all week, that this was the night she was joining some friends for a special dinner program as well as the night that he had agreed to spend some time alone with their young daughter, Stephanie.

Worried about all the work he had to do, the man pleaded with his wife to change her plans saying "Honey, I've got so much to do before morning, there's simply no way I can be with Stephanie and get it all done. Would you please reconsider your plans?" Although sympathetic to his dilemma, his wife continued with her decision to go by saying "I've been looking forward to this night out for a long time and my friends are counting on me being there. Stephanie has also been anxious for an evening with just the two of you. Dinner's in the oven, I'll be back about midnight. I love you. Good-bye."

Hearing her Dad come home, Stephanie ran from her room and jumped into his arms. She was so glad to see him—knowing that this was going to be "their" night together while Mom was away. As they walked into the kitchen to get dinner out of the oven, he began to privately fret and stew about how he was going to occupy and enjoy Stephanie and get his work done at the same time. All through dinner he dwelled on the problem—all the while missing the moments of life with her as she chatted away about her day.

Near the end of the meal, he noticed a pile of stuff by the door leading to the garage where items were placed before being discarded into the trash. He quickly surmised that the pile was the result of his wife's spring cleaning. Among the items was a poster-size picture of the world which apparently had been stuck in an attic or closet for years and no longer had any value. Using a pair

3

of scissors, he cut up the poster into countries, continents and pieces. When Stephanie asked what he was doing, he replied "I've got a big project to do tonight and, while I'm doing it, I though it would be nice if you had one to do too. So, I've created a puzzle for you to work on in your bedroom while I work in the kitchen."

Together, they took all the pieces of the puzzle to Stephanie's bedroom and spread them out on a table. Before returning to the kitchen he said, "We'll get together in an hour and have some popcorn and take a break. If you get stuck before that time and need some help, let me know." Stephanie was thrilled by the opportunity and the challenge of the puzzle and, even though they were in separate rooms, felt like she and her Dad were working along together. He too was thrilled at the creative way he had managed to occupy his daughter so that he could get his office tasks done.

About fifteen minutes after he'd begun his work, he felt a tap on his shoulder from Stephanie. When he asked her what she wanted, she replied "I'm done, Dad." In complete disbelief he responded, "No, you can't be done—it's impossible!" With a big smile on her face she said, "I really am done, Dad; come and see." She took his hand and led him down the hallway to her bedroom where on the table lay the world put back together. Amazed and amused, he sat down on her bed and said, "Stephanie, I thought this was going to be a real tough thing for you to do. How did you do it so quickly?" "It was tough, Dad, until I turned the pieces of the puzzle over and found a picture of a person on the other side. When I put the pieces of the person together and flipped the poster over, the pieces of the world came together, too."

THE STORY OF STEPHANIE is both emotionally moving and freeing. It provides encouragement for each of us to deal with our own inventories and self-defeating behaviors and leave others to do the same with their inner work. It implies that if we take good care of ourselves by going home and honoring our best integrated self, the real or imagined problems external to us have a better chance of either rectifying themselves or becoming more manageable and less bothersome.

Just about always, the clients, students and audiences we're professionally involved with are made up of folks interested in eliminating defeating behaviors and deepening their own spiritual and personal growth. Those that come just to learn therapeutic techniques to help others are gently urged through the Story of Stephanie to, first of all, do a good job in trying to learn the how, what and why of their own defeating behaviors and what must be done to go home by replacing them with more life-generating behaviors. Since such encouragement seems to have served many people well, we urge you to do the same as we now begin to take a look at the nature of defeating behaviors and their inception.

What Are Self-Defeating Behaviors?

GB:
Without getting clinically complicated, I'd like to simply suggest that self-defeating behaviors are any behavior or attitude that a person uses to such an extent that it diminishes the best life possible for that person. They are defeating behaviors because they interfere with our physical health, social and interpersonal connections, mental, emotional and spiritual growth, vocational and educational development as well as our financial stability. They are also responsible for many of life's opportunities being missed, i.e., relationships that could have been, books that could have been written, music that could have been composed, trips that could have been enjoyed, careers that could have flourished, talents that could have blossomed, health that could have lasted, and children who could have been loved and appreciated.

Given this definition, a comprehensive list of self-defeating behaviors would be exhaustive. However, the most common ones that people routinely want to eliminate include the following:

- **Substance Abuse**
- **Inferiority**
- **Excessive worry**
- **Alienation of others**
- **Defensiveness**
- **Negativism**
- **Procrastination**
- **Disorganization**
- **Indecision**

5

- **Perfectionism**
- **Underachievement**
- **Dependency**
- **Poor lifestyle habits (overeating, smoking, etc.)**

When presented with such a list of self-defeating behaviors, it's not unusual for people to identify more than one. In fact, research I've conducted over the years with my clients and students reveal that by the time we reach adulthood we could have developed, practiced and perfected six or more. To make the treatment process manageable, I urge you to identify and work on only one defeating behavior at a time and I specifically request that you chose the one giving you the most negative consequences. In other words, if your appendix is about to rupture, I'm going to dissuade you from a denial-driven focus on chapped lips.

Please also consider looking at the web of self-defeating behaviors in a holistic, interconnected fashion. Eliminating one major defeating behavior pattern often results in the concurrent elimination of others on the list simply because defeating behaviors beget additional defeating behaviors. For those behaviors that remain troublesome, the learning and insight from the successful elimination of the first one can be used as a model and reference point toward eliminating others and promoting life generating behaviors. So, no matter which behavior you isolate and choose to work on, getting the process started will positively impact the whole web.

Most important in the identification process is the encouragement I try to provide toward understanding that we're not perfect and that the closest anyone ever comes to perfection is more than likely on a job application form. Our therapeutic striving, therefore, should be toward progress instead of perfection. This cannot be overemphasized: The work is never really done! With that in mind, I again note that a self-defeating behavior is any attitude or behavior that a person uses "to such an extent" that it diminishes the best life possible. Hence, occasional procrastination, defensiveness, worry, indecision, etc. may not qualify as a behavior worthy of treatment energy. (Recall the continuum mentioned earlier.)

For those folks understandably confused about the selection of a defeating behavior to work on, I offer the following ideas and suggestions. First, reflect upon and consider any consistent feedback you've received over the years such as "You drink too much," or "You always seem so quick-tempered and ready to go off," or "You're the most disorganized person I've ever known," or "Why are you always putting yourself down and reducing your value?" Such comments, when heard over and over again, are often indications or cues of long-standing defeating behavior patterns. If, for example, twelve people independently tell you that you've got a tail, you'd turn your head around a take a look, wouldn't you?

Second, take a look at your family background to determine whether you've taken over the practice of defeating behaviors that were modeled by your parents or other members of our family.

Third, genuinely ask four or five close people in your life to assist you toward making a decision of what self-defeating behavior to work on. Be absolutely sure to pick people who are caring and honest and who won't enable the perpetuation of your behavior or increase your denial of its consequences. If the majority of them suggest the same behavior (which is typically the case), chances are pretty good that it qualifies to be worked on and replaced with a more life-generating behavior.

Fourth, listen deeply to your inner-self, to your internal gyroscope and the signals it sends about your life choices. Then put all this information together and, if you're still confused, it may well be that either 'indecision' or 'confusion' qualifies as the self-defeating behavior to be addressed. You may also appropriately conclude that your life is going along quite smoothly and that you aren't currently practicing any behavior defeating enough to work on. The new section of this edition, "Psychic Gardening" is a tool you can use to help connect to your internal gyroscope and identify your strengths as well as areas you designate as "inner construction zones". I suggest taking yourself through these exercises to help assess, reflect, and in general, "take stock" of your life.

How Do Self-Defeating Behaviors Originate?

GB:
To respond to the question of the inception of defeating behavior patterns requires that I offer a demonstrative verse given to me at a National Ombudsman conference in Monterey, California. Like a psychic kiss, it warmed my insides and attached itself to the same spirit as "Goin' Home." It's an uncomplicated verse requiring only for a moment that you think about your life backwards.

Reverse Living
Author unknown

Life is tough. It takes a lot of your time, all your weekends. And what do you get at the end of it? Death. What a reward.

The Life Cycle is all backwards. You should die first, get it over with - get it out of the way. Then you live for 20 years in an old age home. You get kicked out when you're too young. You get a gold watch. Then you go to work.

You work forty years until you're young enough to enjoy your retirement. You go to college, study, party, make a lot of friends until you're prepared for high school. You go to high school, then grade school. You become a kid, you play, you have no responsibilities. Then you become a precious little baby - and return to the womb.

You spend your last nine months floating and you finish off as a gleam in someone's eye.

So, what happens to these "gleamed" about children? Why is it that as early as elementary school they begin to develop, practice and perfect behaviors which eventually defeat them by restricting, diminishing and often times shortening their lives? To answer this question of origin requires a brief look at the interplay between the developing child and our culture.

Assuming no prenatal damage, each of us is born with the biological hardware of an intact life system composed of integrated parts. These parts, including physical, mental, emotional, social, spiritual, etc. are like seeds waiting to be fertilized and nourished toward growth and harvest. They're naturally hungry and ready to grow to the point that if we could listen to an infant's mind upon coming out of the womb I suspect we'd hear the following concerns and questions: "What's the deal out here? Where's the food? Are there any rules? I'd like to start looking around and traveling - Where's the map?"

As this integrated life system honors its biological hardware and internal gyroscope, it looks to the software of the environment and culture for its physical

8

and psychic food. In addition to nourishing foods, the culture's food supply regretfully contains toxic foods which the young developing seedling is unable to neither distinguish nor digest. In the case of toxic physical food, built-in safeguards come to the rescue. For example, if given a bowl of sand instead of baby food, the internal components of the physical system will naturally and promptly reject the sand because of its inability to create new blood, muscles and cells. But what about the culture's toxic psychic food in the form of attitudes and behaviors? If, as the old saying goes, "You are what you eat," how does the integrated life system respond to the culture's repeated doses of anti-life psychic foods? What are the internal safeguards to deal with this kind of input?

Toxic input from the software of the culture will get received as a psychic shock by the developing life system. And, if that shock is severe and frequent enough to result in a gut full of garbage, the internal unconscious components of the psychic system will naturally scramble for a protective behavioral response to buffer the person from the culture and ease the distress. If the behavioral response works, unconscious conclusions will get formed in favor of keeping it and embracing it as a friend and protective response for reliance upon during future perceived threats from the culture.

One person shared the following story of toxic input reaching a critical mass:

> "When I was in elementary school, the kids on the playground often picked on me, I guess because I was shy and not very interested in sports. One day a girl approached me as I was alone on a swing. She offered to push me and I gratefully accepted her offer of company. After a few minutes, she pushed me off the swing and I flew through the air, landing in the hard dirt. She, and all the other kids watching, pointed and laughed. I stood up and remember thinking: 'That's it. I'll never let myself care about any of them again'. I closed myself off that day, ultimately increasing a lifelong behavior pattern of isolation and subsequent loneliness."

To illustrate this inception process in a more detailed way, I'd like to specifically focus on the behavior of inferiority—from its helpful beginning to its eventual self-defeating betrayal. I've selected inferiority, otherwise known as low self-concept, inferiority complex, low self-esteem, etc., because it's one of the most frequently used defeating behaviors in our culture. Here, in outline form, is an example of the interplay between a child and his culture which fosters its beginning. The child's name is "Joseph"- or "Joe" for short.

Inception of Inferiority

Experiences: ↓	Joe has experiences of being repeatedly criticized for being naturally open and spontaneous.
Resulting Feelings: ↓	As a result, Joe feels hurt, shame, rejection, embarrassment, anxiety, etc.
Relieving Solution: ↓	To offset the pain, Joe withdraws, shuts down, closes up, acts inferior-resulting in a psychic relief.
Psychic Conclusion: ↓	Because of the relief, Joe unconsciously concludes that withdrawal and inferiority are necessary to prevent further hurt and rejection.
Fear: ↓	Based upon this conclusion, Joe fears "If I don't continue to practice withdrawal and inferiority, then I'll just get hurt all over again."
Continued Reliance Upon the New Relieving Behavior:	Joe unconsciously repeats the behavior to offset any further anticipated psychic vulnerability.

This outline shows the sequential series of experiences, feelings, unconscious decisions, conclusions and fears that prompt the beginning of a behavioral pattern of inferiority. The process, in this example, begins with Joe having experiences of being repeatedly criticized for a natural display of openness and spontaneity. I emphasize the words "experiences" and "repeatedly" because, rather than citing a singular trauma moment in history, most people report the origin of their defeating behaviors in terms of multiple painful experiences over periods of time in their life such as Junior High School.

The hurt, shame, embarrassment and anxiety from these repeated experiences gets responded to with an unconscious psychic scramble to find a solution—anything that provides relief which, in Joe's case, turns out to be shutting down, withdrawing and otherwise replacing his original openness and spontaneity with inferior behavior.

10

The psychic relief generated by the discovery of inferiority fosters the development of the psychic conclusion and fear—two forevermore important propellants in the continuation of the behavior. The conclusion purports that the behavior is now necessary to prevent further hurt and rejection; hence Joe's fear, "If I don't continue to practice withdrawal and inferiority, then I'll just get hurt again." Operating unconsciously together, the combination of the conclusion and fear becomes the motivation for further use of the behavior. Rather than being defeating, at this point in time the newly discovered behavior of inferiority seems like a wonderful rescuing friend capable of warding off further threats from the culture to the internal psychic system. However, when used over time past its utility, it eventually backfires and becomes the source of its own defeating consequences.

To further illustrate both the inception and progression of a helpful rescuing behavior that eventually becomes defeating, I'd like to share a little history of two clients and the beginning of a story entitled "Man Overboard" which was donated by my friend, Milt Cudney. Later in the book, I'll return to the story's conclusion. But first, two brief case histories.

The Case of Joanne
Some years ago in a private practice setting, I was waiting for my next client, someone I'd never met. As I looked out the window of my ground floor office, I noticed a woman, somewhere in her mid-thirties, approaching the building. While her appearance in terms of grooming, figure and clothing was tasteful and appealing, the spirit in which she carried herself was both sad and repelling. I remember feeling immediately sorry for her apparent internal suffering which was externally conveyed through a cold, aloof, stuck-up manner. As she passed by my window and entered the building, she reminded me of someone who could have won a contest for Miss Sheet Metal.

A few minutes later, my secretary called to announce the arrival of my new client, Joanne, who turned out to be the same woman I'd just been watching through the window. After the conventional greetings, I asked her "Joanne, how can I assist you?" Her immediate reply was "I'm always lonely." Well, having watched the way she carried herself as she walked up to the building, I already knew that. It doesn't take a clinical wizard to conclude that loneliness is one of the natural consequences of snooty, distancing behavior. After listening to her a little longer, I interrupted to share the observations and feelings I had formed as I watched her approach the building. She wasn't one bit surprised by what I said. In fact, she used my observations to point out that her family, her boss and her friends had all described her with the same words for years! I then said,

"Joanne, you didn't come out of the womb looking like Miss Sheet Metal. Where did this stuck-up stuff come from? Talk to me about your history so we can try to figure out how and why this all began."

Joanne reported being raised in a military family and, as such, frequently moved around the country. She recalled that each time the family moved, she would attempt to reach out, befriend and become a part of the kids in her new neighborhood. Not once, not twice, but repeatedly in many neighborhoods, her efforts failed. Tears came to her eyes as she retrieved the consistent memories of rejection and the concurrent feelings that she didn't qualify, didn't fit, wasn't good enough and wasn't wanted. It hurt me listening to her recollections of sitting on the family porch watching the kids in the neighborhood play as she struggled to make sense out of their exclusion of her. As the tears rolled down her face I said "Joanne, those experiences must have been awful for you because they hurt me just sitting here listening to them. When you're done crying, I'd like to find out what that hurt little girl sitting on all those porches in all those different neighborhoods finally decided to do?" Almost instantly following my question, the tears disappeared as the cold, snooty aloofness reappeared. And, without blinking an eye she responded, "I decided to say 'screw them;' if they ever want to be with me, they're going to have to work at it and earn it."

Behaviorally, the "screw them" remark took the form of a mask of arrogant steel to both hide the hurt and prevent her from being penetrated again. It worked! It provided immediate relief and, as such, got filed in the unconscious portion of her mind as a friend to call upon again which, unfortunately, she did for the next 25 years. What had been the solution for the child was now the problem for the adult. What temporarily worked to prevent further pain and rejection as a child on the porch now guaranteed it as an adult. Joanne had become the adult child, continuing to rely upon a childhood behavior long after its utility. Although it had backfired years ago and become completely self-defeating, Joanne was unconsciously terrified to surrender it out of fear that she'd once again be vulnerable.

The Case of Bob

The second case example I'd like to provide for illustration purposes comes from a conversation I had years ago with author and therapist Earnie Larsen during which he shared the story of a client who I'll call Bob. As I recall the story, Earnie asked Bob during their first session why he wanted therapy to which Bob responded "because I just rammed a semi-trailer truck." Perplexed at the answer,

12

Earnie asked for clarification and was again told "because I just rammed a truck." You'll note here that the verb being used is "rammed" rather than "I just had an accident with a big truck." When asked for more details, Bob described the semi-driver as coming in on a freeway entrance ramp and cutting too close to the front of Bob's car. So he rammed him! Earnie then asked Bob if he'd ever done this before and was told "Yep, three times." Well, it isn't a case of higher math to figure out that, at the very least, Bob was suffering from a shortage of ideas on how to deal with encroaching trucks. And this "road rage" was probably only a symptom of deeper difficulties. So the clinical question became, "Where did this kind of behavior come from?"

As Earnie shared the story, by the time Bob was seven years old, his father was a chronic alcoholic. Bob recalled the many times he and his mother had been beaten by his father and the accumulation of painful memories coming from those beatings. On one especially painful occasion, he remembered hiding and cowering under the dining room table as his father, in an alcoholic rage, pounded his mother against the dining room wall. Her screams and cries for help left Bob feeling helpless, terrified and full of shame from which he resolved to never, ever get in a position where he could be pushed around, bullied and made a fool of again. Shortly thereafter, the lessons learned from the experiences of helplessly, shamefully cowering under the table resulted in Bob developing, practicing and perfecting a defensive hostile behavioral exterior which years later took the form of ramming semis and reaffirming the age-old notion that "hurt people hurt people." Although 40 at the time, it was really a seven year old adult child driving Bob's car into those trucks.

The therapeutic challenge with both Bob and Joanne, as with all people wishing to eliminate self-defeating behaviors, is to understand the terrible struggle and tug-of-war between letting the behavior go and holding onto it for dear life. Often times I'll help clients visualize this struggle by using a map of the United States as a metaphor for change. As we begin therapy, I'll place the client in Texas with a goal of getting to Maine. Texas represents distress, grief, loneliness, unhappiness, misery, out-of-sync, fractionated, you name it. Maine, on the other hand, represents holistic, together, self-actualized, in sync, congruent, joyful, serenity. Maine is going home! The goal of therapy is to get the person from Texas to Maine without detouring and screwing around in Las Vegas, New Orleans or the upper peninsula of Michigan. Just about always, however, clients have mixed feelings about the trip and, although they may desperately want to get to Maine, they're also frightened to go and will therefore attempt to derail the process. Counseling and psychology books, at least the ones I read years ago, call this phenomenon "approach avoidance, resistance to therapy" or "the resistant client." What's being resisted on the journey is prompted by the unconscious conclusion and fears which purport that the original (now self-defeating) behavior is still necessary to prevent anticipated psychic vulnerability. So why in the world would anybody want to leave Texas, go to Maine and dump such a behavioral buddy? The answer, simply put, is because Texas now only creates pain! Joanne's misery and loneliness from years of wearing her sheet metal mask has finally become unbearable. Likewise, Bob's chronic defensive hostility has cost him dearly in terms of relationships, jobs, health and legal fees. While perceived as a friend at inception, these behaviors have now betrayed their owners and become self-defeating to the point where their consistent and accumulating resulting grief makes the trip to Maine at least worth trying.

In concluding this "Leaving Home" section of the book, I want to summarize and re-emphasize that self-defeating behaviors initially come to us disguised as friends bearing the gift of protection and psychic relief from toxic and repeated painful experiences from our culture. To the degree that they're successful, they get stored in the unconscious fire station of our mind ready to roll at the next hint of smoke—even when there's no fire. The conclusion and fears derived from the behavior's initial capacity to bring relief promote an unhealthy and unnecessary reliance upon the behavior's continued use which eventually backfires by creating the very problems the behavior was originally designed to extinguish. Hence, what was a sanctuary in the beginning has now become a prison which separates the person from their best inner self and life-generating choices. As such, they have abandoned their psychic and spiritual home and begun to wander.

Man Overboard (Cudney & Hardy, 1991)
Part I

After years of hard work, a successful businessman finally took an ocean cruise he had been dreaming of his entire life. He spent his days walking the deck of the huge ocean liner smelling the fresh sea air and lifting his eyes to contemplate the vast and clear horizon. One day, however, a violent storm blew up suddenly. Before the man could take shelter, a blast of wind blew him against the deck railing. A second gale caught him before he could gain his balance and he tumbled over the top of the railing. As he fell overboard, he reached out to grab something—anything he could hang onto. And luckily, he caught the tine of a heavy anchor suspended from a link chain on the side of the ship. He grasped the anchor with both hands and squeezed its tines until his knuckles turned white. As the storm winds buffeted him from side to side, he clung to the anchor holding on for dear life.

At last the storm abated and, although he still clung to the anchor that had saved his life, he was able to relax a bit. Soon enough, he thought, someone on the cruise ship would notice his absence and send a crew out to rescue him. He did not know, however, that the chain from which the anchor hung had been damaged in the storm. One of its links was badly eroded and the battering force of the wind had caused it to crack.

The sun had just reappeared when, finally, the damaged link gave way. Both the anchor and the terrified man who clung to it fell into the ocean and began to sink. As he plunged underwater, the sinking man had only one thought... "This anchor saved my life," he told himself, "If I let go of it, I'm sure to die."

— To be continued

15

Wandering and Getting Lost

GIVEN THE WAY our culture's rigged up with its smorgasbord of both life-generating and toxic psychic foods, it's no surprise that many of us, by the time we become adults, have developed to perfection any number of self-defeating behaviors. Most of us have no idea where they came from or how and why we keep them going. But, if we listen deeply enough to our internal gyroscope and its life-enhancing signals, we eventually conclude that we're lost and something's wrong. And, when that "something's wrong" generates enough grief to bring us to our own personal bottom, we surrender and ask for help.

By the time a genuine request for help is made, most defeating behaviors are firmly entrenched and operating below the level of consciousness. Counseling, personal coaching, and self-help work, therefore, become consciousness raising experience to let in the light. To illustrate this idea in connection with the Texas to Maine road map, we routinely share the following picture of the human mind with our clients.

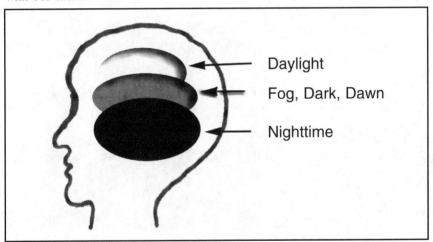

Daylight

Fog, Dark, Dawn

Nighttime

Figure 1

The illustration in Figure 1 reveals the minimal degree to which we operate out of our conscious mind and the disproportionate influence of the nighttime of our mind. We tell our clients and audiences that the growth experience of traveling from Texas to Maine is essentially a process of getting the why, the how, and the consequences of their self-defeating behavior into the light of day so that fresh and more appropriate choices can be made to replace those currently being driven by the nighttime of their minds. We tell them that this process of "going home" by eliminating and replacing long-standing defeating behavior patterns is similar to taking a gentle acting laxative and that the process to flush out psychic constipation requires time, patience, faith and work. Growth and change involve the time-release of experiences, feelings, memories and events from the nighttime, fog and dusk of the mind into daylight where the old and now phony conclusion and mythical fears can be accurately tested against reality.

"When you come to the edge of all the light you know, and are about to step off into the darkness of the unknown, faith is knowing one of two things will happen: There will be something solid to stand on or you will be taught how to fly." -...Barbara J. Winter

HOW SELF-DEFEATING BEHAVIORS ARE MAINTAINED AND PERPETUATED

GB:
Once they've been conceived, self-defeating behaviors are thereafter put into operation and perpetuated through a sequential series of steps. Each time the behavior is activated reveals an orderly progression of the ingredients in Figure 2.

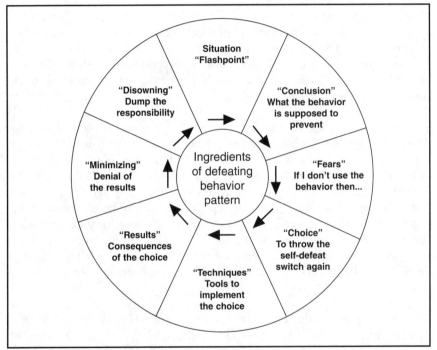

Figure 2

Each of these eight ingredients will now be sequentially discussed in order to later show how they all work together to perpetuate the self-defeating behavior of inferiority which originated with Joe in Part I of this book.

1. Situation (Flashpoint)
Self-defeating behaviors are not practiced 24 hours a day, seven days a week. Rather, they are reserved like fire trucks for those moments, situations and circumstances that appear to signal their need. The initial process of therapy, therefore, requires the identification of situational flashpoints which sound the alarm.

This can rather easily be accomplished through a focus on where, when, with whom and under what circumstances the behavior is typically used. This process, by itself, is consciousness-raising because so many owners of self-defeating behaviors inaccurately believe that their behavior is always present, i.e., "I'm always depressed, I'm always disorganized, I always procrastinate," etc. But, when examined closely, these behaviors of depression, disorganization and procrastination are, like all self-defeating behaviors, put into operation selectively instead of continually.

Years ago a college student came to see me for counseling and when I asked "How can I help you?" he replied, "I'm always depressed." "Are you depressed right now?" I asked. "Yes, I'm always depressed." "Were you depressed 10 minutes ago when you were waiting for me in the reception room?" With mild impatience he replied, "Look, I've already told you twice, but I'll say it again, I'm always depressed."

Although the student was convinced that he was always depressed, I wasn't. So, I empathized with his irritation and asked him to stick with me until I could get more clarity on what he was trying to tell me. I also told him that, at times, I was sort of a slow learner and that, as my teacher of his life, I'd appreciate his patience in answering my questions. I then said something like this: "Let's see, you're depressed now and you were depressed while you waited for me in the lobby; were you depressed while you were driving here for your counseling appointment?" With muffled irritation and a growing desire to find a different therapist, he slowly and more loudly (wondering if I was hearing impaired) replied "Yes, I'm *always* depressed." "Were you depressed an hour ago?" I shot back.

His facial response to this last question revealed a combination of astonishment and bewilderment. Like a psychological arrow striking its target, my question hit home. With complete amazement he responded, "An hour ago I was taking a shower and I don't think I was depressed." "How about an hour and 15 minutes ago?" I asked. "Let's see," he replied, "just before my shower, I fed the dog and I wasn't depressed then either." "And before the dog?" I asked. "Before the dog, I spent an hour shooting baskets with some guys in the neighborhood and I wasn't depressed then either!" "How about three hours ago, were you depressed then?" I asked. "Three hours ago it was awful," he replied, "I was really depressed."

The purpose of this initial tracking was to bust the automatic and inaccurate belief that the client was "always depressed." When challenged on this notion, he was able to see that his depression was really a behavior he periodically used in certain situations and not in others. Getting this awareness into his conscious mind helped him own the behavior as something he "did" rather than continue to view it as an unfortunate condition imposed upon him. It also paved the way for subsequent questions of how and why such a behavior was seen as necessary.

2. Conclusion (*Why* the behavior is used)
When presented with flashpoint situations internally reminiscent of the threat the behavior originally relieved, the conclusion gets withdrawn from the conclusion closet of the unconscious mind. The conclusion is always framed in such a way as to make (what has now become) the self-defeating behavior seem like a smart thing to do again in order to prevent anticipated psychic vulnerability. It says, "I helped you before and I'll do it again. So, follow me."

3. Fears (*Why* the behavior is used)
Hand-in-glove with the conclusion come the fears. As long as the behavior is deemed essential by the psychic conclusion to guard against assumed danger, it will naturally be frightening to be without the behavior in whatever the flashpoint situation may be. Therefore, in the owner's mind, the fear takes on an "if-then" reality: "If I don't continue to practice inferiority, procrastination, substance abuse, alienation, disorganization, etc., then I'll just get hurt all over again." It is the combination of the psychic conclusion and fears working together that provides the reason for the perpetuation of the behavior. Until and unless the two of them are brought into consciousness and challenged for the accuracy of their claims, they will continue to direct the owner toward further use of the behavior and its defeating consequences.

4. Choice (Throw the self-defeat switch)
Prompted by the historical and now phony wisdom of the conclusion and fears, the owner once again throws the self-defeat switch and relies upon the old behavior for use in the new flashpoint situation. Because of years of practice, this process is so fast that most people fail to recognize that they even make a choice—preferring instead to genuinely believe that the self-defeating behavior "just happened again."

5. Techniques (*How* the behavior is implemented)
But, the throwing of the self-defeat switch and the implementation of the self-defeating behavior doesn't "just happen." When this process is examined and freeze-framed through therapy, it becomes apparent that the owner actually calls

upon a handful of favorite tools or techniques to set the behavior into motion. Acting like gears in an assembly line or ingredients in a recipe, these techniques actuate the behavior and guarantee its manifestation.

In the simplest sense, techniques are any kind of thought or action that help promote and deliver the self-defeating behavior. They can be privately internal or visibly external. Examples of those internally generated include dwelling upon past hurts, anticipating negative results, creating unrealistic expectations and distorting feedback. External techniques are observable actions which assist in the implementation of the behavior.

Examples include chronic lateness, lying, failing to meet obligations, inappropriate laughing or crying, etc. Most people use a favorite combination of internal and external techniques each time they do their behavior. Without techniques, the behavior couldn't be implemented; hence the importance of identifying and isolating them in the therapeutic process.

6. Results (Consequences of the behavior)
When someone uses a self-defeating behavior over a long period of time they get psychically constipated and, sooner or later, their mind and body gets presented with a bill. Results are the inevitable "fallout" from practicing a self-defeating behavior and the reason the behavior can appropriately be identified as defeating. Without results, there would be no motivation to change. Results are the physical, mental, emotional, spiritual, financial, vocational and social consequences of continuing a behavior long after its utility. As such, and if they are allowed to do so, they become the driving force to get out of Texas and head for Maine.

7. Minimizing (Denial of the results)
If we listen to the results and honor them, they become instructional toward our journey home. If we don't, the lessons go unlearned and the bill to our mind and body gets more expensive. Minimizing is a process of reducing the severity of the results. This denial or downplaying of the pain presents itself in many ways. Common ones include:
- keeping too busy to face the results
- comparing oneself to another person who is worse off
- making a joke out of the results
- numbing oneself to the pain of the results through medications or drugs and alcohol
- distorting the results to make them somehow seem beneficial
- adapting to the results by building a way of life around them

These minimizing strategies accomplish two things. First, they assist the mission of the conclusion and fears toward further use of the self-defeating behavior. Second, they deceive the owner into believing that the behavior's not so bad after all and, consequently, the motivation for the trip to Maine gets diminished or outright cancelled.......perhaps for the umpteenth time.

Continuing the practice of a self-defeating behavior by honoring the old conclusion and fears and then minimizing the consequential damage can be visualized as a ride on a one-way elevator—going down (Figure 3). The ultimate decision for the passenger is one of establishing their own personal bottom floor where they decide to get off. The higher the floor, the less the defeating results. The lower—the more! While the internal gyroscope repeatedly sends life-enhancing signals to get off the elevator, minimizing the results encourages the owner to continue the behavior and the ride. So, down it goes.

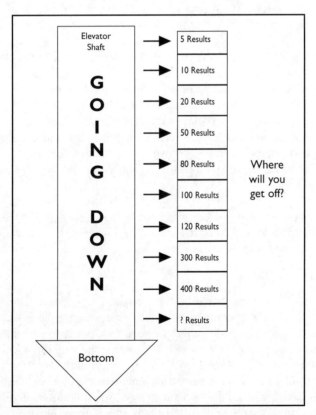

Figure 5

8. Disowning (Become blameless and helpless)
The final ingredient in the process of maintaining and perpetuating a self-defeating behavior is the refusal to take personal responsibility for its continued existence. Disowning is a mental process of blaming other people, things, events or circumstances in order to explain or justify the behavior. It is a subtle way of deceiving the owner into believing that the behavior is not of their choosing and that they are, therefore, helpless, powerless victims.

Encouragement for disowning is rampantly available from our culture which not only provides the initial toxic input for the inception of self-defeating behaviors but also the ongoing models to perpetuate them by shifting blame and responsibility. Day after day our news media report examples of people blaming to become blameless to the point where it's now fashionable to become a victim. Although there are, of course, a horrendous number of real victims, many people are enabled to feign victimization through the popular process of disowning responsibility for their own defeating choices.

To leave Texas and get to Maine requires a personal ownership of the continuing self-defeating choice. If it's not owned as a personal decision someone makes, it cannot be eliminated and replaced. If the behavior is seen as something somebody's 'got' rather than something somebody 'does', the person will remain helpless and stuck. Therapy, therefore, requires an ongoing effort to assist the owner of a self-defeating behavior toward dismantling disowning and increasing ownership. Remember, we're not consciously being sneaky or deceptive here, but instead protective of our self-defeating behavior at an unconscious level.

The following examples of disowning statements are offered to illustrate the very subtle and tricky nature of the disowning process. They are donated from clients I've worked with over the years:

• "My Mind Went Blank"

This disowning statement was used by a bright, academically talented college student to explain his continuing poor performance on college examinations. Rather than own up to the techniques he used to produce low exam scores, i.e. procrastination, skipping class, excessive partying, studying the wrong material, showing up the wrong day for exams, etc., he chose to disown it onto his mind which "goes blank" during exams. He wanted understanding and sympathy from me as well as a referral to a neurologist to see if he was wired up screwy. I suggested instead that we take a look at how he blanks his mind in test situations and what the blanking is designed to accomplish. I told him "Your mind doesn't just go and 'blank itself' and if you keep talking like that you're going to stay stuck and helpless." By breaking the pattern of this disowning language, the student was eventually able to own his defeating choice and techniques to perform poorly on exams so that we could then focus on the driving conclusion and fears underneath.

• "My Lack of Self-Discipline Makes Me Overeat"

This was a frequently used disowning statement by a client who's self-defeating behavior was overeating. Rather than recognizing the techniques which propelled her to the refrigerator, junk food and sweets, she chose to disown her behavior onto something called "self-discipline" which she envisioned as an empty reservoir inside of her. When the techniques of how she repeatedly relapsed off her diet were finally brought into the light of her conscious mind, the underlying conclusion and fears supporting her excessive weight became available to the therapy process.

• "I Got Depressed"

The self-defeating behavior of depression can be disowned by characterizing the depression as an "it" that somebody's "got." This behavior can and should be differentiated from chemically induced or clinical depression by looking at the context and frequency of its use. Self-defeating depression is a behavior that the owner uses in selective flashpoint situations to an assumed advantage dictated by underlying psychic conclusions and fears. It is not to be confused with appropriate grief or sadness from dealing with life on life's terms which sometimes includes harsh and painful events. When used to disown a defeating depression, "I got depressed" sounds like "a big cloud of depression came by and plopped on me." What's being disowned in this statement is the user's contribution to the depression being experienced. A thorough look at the techniques being employed to generate the depression is essential to assist in the dismantling of disowning and the empowerment of ownership. Once this is accomplished, the behavior can accurately be seen as a choice instead of an affliction thereby opening the door to the underlying conclusions and fears and subsequent life-generating choices.

• "I Get Relapses"

This phrase is commonly used to disown repetition of a self-defeating behavior. The very nature of the words "I get relapses" implies that the owner is powerless over a behavior that strikes without warning. To change this disowning statement to ownership language requires an understanding that "relapse" is on

27

active verb and, as such, something somebody "does" rather than something somebody "gets." We get strep throat, diarrhea and the flu—but relapses are actions we create. To emphasize this point of ownership, I frequently ask clients to share how they do their relapses. Sometimes I'll even ask if they wouldn't mind relapsing in front of me in the office so that we can both get a better idea of how they create it.

- "Something came over me"
- "It's God's wish, that's why it happens"
- "My temper got the best of me"
- "It's the Dutch in me"
- "My emotions took over"
- "It's my wife's fault, she brings out the worst in me"
- "It's my DNA"

All of these disowning remarks are designed to pass the trash in order to free the owner from responsibility for their self-defeating behavior. It's important to note that sometimes the targets of disowning have some merit. For example, it's easy to recognize and be impacted by real injustices from social, political or economic inequities. But when these are blamed disproportionately in order to justify defeating choices, disowning has taken over and reduced the owner to a helpless victim.

Some examples of disowning are so absurd that they become comical. Through a police officer friend of mine I was able to collect the following examples of disowning statements from people pulled over for clearly exceeding the speed limit:

- "Officer, my wife is going to get pregnant tonight and I want to be there when she does."
- "I was speeding to get away from my mother-in-law."
- "Officer, my car is so light that the wind blew it over the speed limit. Honest to God."
- One man said he had "a right to speed" to make up for lost time in a construction zone. His average speed, he insisted, was 55 mph for the past hour.
- Another man nailed for speeding told police he was driving fast because he was furious that his wife had just gotten a ticket for speeding.
- A woman with a dead serious expression looked at the apprehending officer and simply said that she was speeding to keep up with the cars behind her.

People can also fragment their body and mind into parts for disowning purposes. One of my favorite examples comes from a story Milt Cudney shared with

28

me about his early professional life as a Jr. High School counselor. As I recall the story, a prematurely developed heavy-chested girl got permission from her teacher to go to the bathroom. As she walked down the corridor of the building to the girl's bathroom she was passed by a boy on his way to the boy's room. Seeing the size of her chest and the emptiness of the corridor, he decided to seize the opportunity and touch one of her breasts. She immediately reported the culprit to the school principal who promptly ushered him to Milt— the counselor. After about half an hour of unsuccessful lying and denying, the boy realized that his explanation was going nowhere. And so he pleadingly looked at Milt and said, "Mr. Cudney, you're going to have a tough time believing this but, honest to God, when I walked by that girl my arm just reached right out and touched her."

When people disown their behavior onto a body part like this example, it's almost always accompanied with a plea for understanding and sympathy for their uniquely personal misfortune at having an uncontrollable arm, fist, foot, penis, mind, mouth, etc. They'll even request a referral to a neurologist for an MRI or another specialist for a prophylactic devise to keep the berserk body part in check and they'll outright envy you and your loved ones for being blessed with body parts that work the way they're supposed to.

If a self-defeating behavior continues to be viewed as an "it," "condition," or "affliction," the owner will remain handcuffed and helpless toward replacing the behavior with a more life-enhancing choice. Disowning perceptions and language, therefore, must be changed to ownership. Hence, the man who says "I got depressed" will need help in understanding how he depresses himself. The woman who says "I get disorganized" must come to understand the techniques she uses to create disorganization. The person who says "I get paralyzed when asked to speak in front of groups" will need assistance in discovering how the paralysis is self-generated. And, the person who disowns the self-defeating behavior of overeating on "hunger attacks" will have to come to terms with how and under what circumstances (flashpoint situations) the hunger is created. Disowning keeps a person stuck. Ownership restores power, responsibility and the opportunity for change.

An understanding of the contribution of these eight ingredients (flashpoint situation, conclusion, fears, choice, techniques, results, minimizing and disowning) toward the repetition of a self-defeating pattern is essential to get from Texas to Maine. Each one of them serves as a benchmark on the road map toward going home. The owner of the behavior must realize that it's chosen for use only in particular situations and that it's driving force comes from a historical combination of a psychic conclusion and fears that once upon a time made the behavior seem like a smart thing to do. It must further be realized that each time the behavior is put into operation requires a handful of techniques which serve as implementing tools or gears in an assembly line to produce the self-defeating product. To get rid of the behavior typically requires a complete acknowledgment of its past, present and anticipated damaging results. Any effort to minimize or deny such results will predictably reduce the motivation for change. Finally, the behavior and its perpetuation through these ingredients must be owned as something the user does instead of disowned as a condition or affliction.

Self-defeating behaviors are former friends that eventually betray us. Although they came into our lives and rescued us during a time of need, their helpfulness has long since passed to the point where they now create the very grief they originally eliminated. As owners of these former friendly behaviors, we don't understand the betrayal. And, because of the safety benefits falsely purported by the conclusion and fears, we don't trust our lives without the behavior. So, we hold on tight and resist any suggestion, opportunity or attempt to let the behavior go.

A young adult shared his story of hanging onto compulsive perfectionism as a way of finding comfort and security:

> "To someone on the outside, someone disorganized, struggling in school, or who always seems to get into trouble for their spontaneous lifestyle, it may not seem like I have a problem at all. However, I feel that my worry and need for life to be a pre-mapped, smooth road is holding me back from many exciting experiences. Without taking chances, reasonable risks, or being spontaneous, I miss opportunities to experience many incredible things. Most importantly, I haven't allowed myself to become vulnerable or to make the choices, changes and mistakes I feel are necessary to fully develop into an adult person".

HOW A SELF-DEFEATING BEHAVIOR IS IMPLEMENTED

GB:

Returning now to Joe and the self-defeating behavior of inferiority, let's take a look at the process he uses to put the behavior into operation in new moments in life. The illustration in Figure 4 is designed to visually and sequentially outline the implementation process by mapping out six of the eight ingredients. The remaining two, minimizing and disowning, will be discussed later.

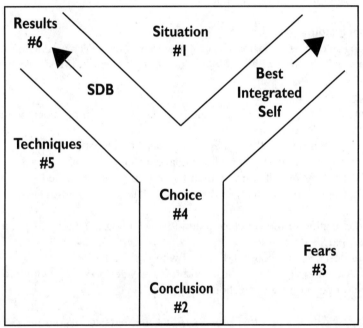

Figure 4

Joe has come for counseling because of the accumulated grief associated with his long-standing behavior of inferiority which he unconsciously began years ago as a helpful response to toxic and painful experiences from his environment. Although the behavior relieved the pain then, it has long since backfired and lost its utility. But, rather than testing and trusting himself in new moments in life without the behavior, he assumes his continued vulnerability and the behavior's subsequent necessity for psychic safety and insurance. Like the story

31

of the Man Overboard, Joe clings to the anchor as he sinks deeper and deeper into its consequences. Having abandoned the signals of wisdom from his own internal gyroscope to surrender the behavior, he is confused, lost and wants help.

1. Situation

Like all owners of self-defeating behaviors, Joe's use of inferiority is reserved and implemented selectively. It is not used continuously. In the illustration (see Figure 5), the flashpoint situation where he'll use the behavior is a party to which Joe has accepted an invitation. On the way to the party, he begins to question and mistrust the acceptability of his best-integrated self.

2. Conclusion

Reaching into the conclusion closet, Joe retrieves the psychic conclusion from long ago which says "withdrawal and inferiority prevent hurt and rejection."

3. Fears

Continued faith in the accuracy of the old conclusion then prompts an immediate flurry of "if-then" fears:
- "If I reach out to others, then I'll just become embarrassed."
- "If I try to be social, then I'll just make a fool of myself."
- "If I extend myself warmly, then I'll end up getting ridiculed."
- "If I open up personally and share who I am, then I'll just get rejected."

The combination of the conclusion and fears working together tells Joe that:
- the party's dangerous.
- his best self isn't equipped to deal with the danger.
- he ought to, therefore, put his old friends, 'inferiority' and 'withdrawal' into operation for protection.

What's fascinating about this process is that the fears are all presupposed and imagined. Joe hasn't even stepped foot into the party, yet he's already got himself scared about its mythical dangers. Not one of his protections is helpful. Consequently, he'll need to abandon his best social skills, attitudes and relationship talents in favor of assumed protection through what once worked so long ago..............withdrawal and inferiority. Hence, the solution has become the problem.

4. Choice

Having made the party dangerous and himself vulnerable, Joe flips the self-defeat switch and begins the process of implementing inferiority as he enters the party environment.

5. Techniques

Internal and external techniques carry out his choice. Like gears in an assembly line, each one compliments the other to ultimately produce the self-defeating behavior. Without them, the behavior couldn't survive. Not long after entering the party, Joe initiates the first (internal) technique of negative self-talk concluding "I have nothing in common with any of these people." Shortly thereafter, he begins the second (internal) technique of comparing himself to other people at the party in such a way as to come off unworthy. This is an extremely popular technique with those who practice inferiority. It involves a very selective scan of the party to identify and focus upon someone who, compared to Joe, is wealthier, better dressed, better built, more popular, more liked, etc. These perceived gifts and attributes of the other person are then magnified and dwelled upon until Joe feels completely worthless and advances to the next technique (external) of finding a corner in the party where he can stand alone, pout and generally look unpleasant and unavailable.

While clinging to the corner of the room, someone approaches Joe and engages him in conversation which includes a genuine compliment about the sweater he's wearing. Instead of graciously accepting the remark and using the opportunity to further the conversation, Joe dismisses the person's comments by saying "It's an old sweater. I got it in a garage sale and if you look at it closer, you'll see that it's got holes in it." This (internal and external) technique of distorting feedback and minimizing honest compliments along with the subsequent (external) techniques of acting shy, avoiding eye contact, mumbling and cutting himself down before others get a chance to all serve the purpose of advancing the self-imposed production of the behavior of inferiority. These techniques also illustrate the powerful role of a phenomenon called "self-fulfilling prophecy". Essentially, we experience what we expect to experience because we, to a great extent, create our own expected results.

6. Results

Instead of offering protection, the use of inferiority at the party guarantees the very results the behavior was supposed to guard against. Rather than preventing hurt and rejection as the conclusion and fears promised, Joe's display of inferiority throughout the party produces feelings of embarrassment, discomfort and anxiety as well as a self-report of "looking stupid, getting ridiculed and having no fun." When the implementation process is examined in Figure 5, the folly of

Joe's self-defeating behavior becomes obvious. What the conclusion (#2) and fears (#3) purport is the exact opposite of what the behavior of inferiority actually delivers through its results (#6).

Hence, what used to be a rescuing friend for Joe has again betrayed him turning the sanctuary of long ago into today's prison. But until and unless the self-defeating results (#6) are brought into his conscious mind and used to rescind the phony conclusion, Joe will more than likely increase his use of the behavior in a misguided effort to protect himself from its growing consequences.

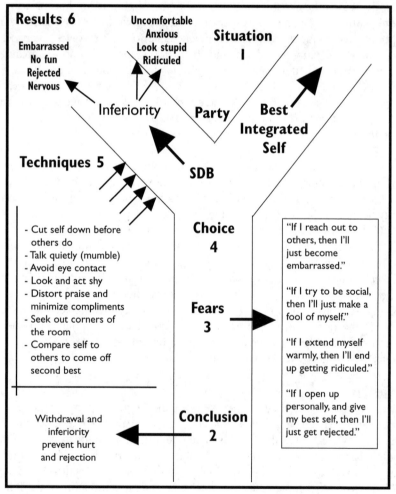

Figure 5

The two ingredients of the implementation cycle omitted from Figures 4 and 5 are Minimizing and Disowning. Each one plays a crucial role toward enabling Joe to not only continue his self-defeating behavior, but to do it even more.

Minimizing

The motivation for Going Home is driven by the behavior's consequences. If those consequences or results are not painful enough, the trip to Maine gets delayed and the downward elevator ride continues. At this point in the worsening progression of Joe's self-defeating behavior, two opposing forces operate simultaneously. The one force is his internal guidance system or gyroscope which sends repeated signals to surrender the damaging behavior and to once again trust in his best integrated self instead of the conclusion and mythical fears. The opposing force is the combination of conclusion and mythical fears which continue to characterize the behavior as essential insurance for psychic safety.

If the conclusion and fears win the battle of the forces, it will then be necessary for Joe to minimize or downplay the severity of the behavior's results (like putting perfume on a pig – the pig still stinks). Hence, when confronted in therapy with the actual consequences of his latest use of inferiority, i.e., being embarrassed, having no fun, getting rejected, feeling nervous, being uncomfortable, feeling anxious, looking stupid and getting ridiculed, Joe immediately begins the minimizing process by:

1. Comparing himself to other people at the party whom he thought were having a worse time;
2. Ridiculing or belittling the noticeable real fun people were actually having at the party;
3. Making the party unimportant, i.e., "I've gotten along fine up to now; who needs these people or this kind of party?"

When pressed a little further in the therapy session about his miserable experience at the party, Joe again honors the conclusion and fears by replying "Yep, I knew this party was going to be dangerous; I should have thought twice about going. In fact, next time I get an invitation, I'll just stay home. Heck with them." This complete failure to recognize and own up to the fact that his own behavior of inferiority produced the misery does nothing but insure and increase his use of it again.

Disowning

To complete the implementation cycle, Joe must now disown responsibility for the behavior and turn himself into its victim rather than its owner and perpetuator. To accomplish this, he creates multiple targets to blame:

• **"It's a family trait; I inherited it from my Dad. He had an inferiority complex, too!"**

What Joe's saying by this remark is "no wonder I got it; after all Dad had it." Disowning language like this turns inferiority into an "it" he's "got" rather than a behavioral choice he makes. While it may be true that his Dad also practiced inferiority, it's not in the family blood or his brothers and sisters would also be afflicted. Current psychological research suggests that some traits may be influenced by genetic inheritance; still it's unlikely that this disowning statement carries the weight that Joe assigns it.

• **"If I would have been raised better, I wouldn't have this inferiority."**

Here again, through the use of the word "have," the behavior of inferiority is characterized as an affliction rather than a decision that's made time and time again in selective flashpoint situations like the party. Picking on the way we were raised by our family is a very popular disowning target and, while it's accurate that many families and environments are dysfunctional and damaging, eventually we must take ownership for our contribution to the continuation of the problems they began. Not long ago, a client of mine spent the entire first hour of our therapy session blaming his mother for all the problems he was experiencing in life. While I was initially sympathetic and attentive, by the end of the hour I felt a sense of boredom as he continued ranting about his awful mother. At the beginning of our next session, he started in again and probably would have spent the whole hour blaming if I hadn't interrupted to suggest that it all seemed unproductive and that my listening to it any further would only serve to enable his disownership.

Startled by my response, he requested permission for "just five more minutes" of blame during which he once again whipped himself into a full fever about his monster mom. When the five minutes were up I asked him if he'd ever seen other therapists about this problem with his mother to which he replied "Yes, six different therapists over a period of the last ten years." Out of curiosity, I then asked the whereabouts of his mother to which he responded, "Well, she's been dead for seventeen years," to which I responded "Well, do you suppose you've played any part in keeping this mess going since she crossed over?"

If even half of what he had told me about his mother was true, I had no problem believing that she, indeed, had been a world-class creature undeserving of a motherhood hall-of-fame award. But, whatever problems she had contributed to his life were long ago taken over and perpetuated by him through his defeating behavior, techniques, minimizing and disowning.

- **"It's my weak ego, that's why I don't mix well."**

Whenever I hear this remark with a disowning tone I ask my clients to point to their ego and tell me "when it was last strong and muscular." They just look at me in bewilderment until they get the point that this is just disowning psychobabble.

- **"My tongue froze up. It always does in social situations."**

When Joe laid this one on me I replied, "Joseph, your tongue isn't an independent unit running on batteries. It just doesn't go and freeze itself. It's your tongue; you own it and you alone operate it!"

- **"This inferiority is imbedded in me. It's just part of me."**

Claiming the behavior as a part of his body is Joe's last disowning stance. Like the preceding statements, it's designed to explain away his responsibility for its continued existence and to get him off the hook of ownership. To rehook him, I asked "If this behavior is imbedded in you, how does it jump out of bed with you in all the other situations in your life where you don't use it?" Questions like this are essential toward moving Joe away from victimization and into ownership where he can feel empowered instead of helpless.

So, there's the story of Joe and his disabling behavior of inferiority. Begun years ago as an unconscious helpful response to the destabilizing forces in his family, it has now become completely self-imposed and self-defeating. By continuing to rely upon it, he denies himself the choices from his best integrated self and their corresponding potential results of joy, productivity and serenity.

Man Overboard

Part II

....*As the anchor sank deeper and deeper into the ocean, the man who had been thrown overboard still continued to cling to it. He knew that he was sinking fast, but he also knew that hanging onto the anchor had saved his life. So, he held his breath and allowed the weight of the anchor to carry him toward the ocean floor. He was aware that he was in danger, but the anchor, which had saved him once, might miraculously save him again.*

"This really isn't so bad," the man thought to himself. "It's kind of pleasant down here, once you get used to it. The water's warm and there's a real sense of peace and quiet. It's not like being on a ship where a storm can come upon you in a flash and throw you overboard."

Finally the anchor came to rest on the ocean floor. The man who still clung to it was having difficulty holding his breath. His lungs burned and his head filled with pressure. "What am I going to do to get out of this mess?" he asked himself, believing all the while that sooner or later a member of the ship's crew would appear to rescue him.

— To be continued

Goin' Home

STEPS IN THE CHANGE PROCESS

"In the midst of winter I found within me an invincible summer"
.... Albert Camus

"I saw an angel in the marble and I chiseled till I set him free"
.... Michelangelo

GB:

IT'S TIME TO GO HOME. It's time to put the fears aside and trust in our best integrated self and give it an opportunity to once again serve us as it was originally designed to do. It's time to recognize that our history should be a guide post instead of a hitching post and that if we make the present good, the past will take care of itself. It's time to get back into balance by honoring the best feelings, attitudes and choices that lie deep within waiting for us to capitalize on their wisdom. It's time to reclaim the spiritual journey that was derailed when we took on our self-defeating behaviors and to enjoy the awakening back into the unity, the oneness and spirit that permeates all things. It's time to rediscover and thereby recover home—that place within us that's not in form, not in time and not in space. It's just there—waiting and beckoning.

"A Chinese proverb reads, 'If you don't know where you are going, you won't know when you get there.' An addendum to this is: Even if you do know where you are going, you can get there sooner and with less wear and tear if you know how to travel. The journey of self-discovery and self-creation is the most exciting, challenging, exhilarating, confounding journey you will ever take. It can be fraught with wrong turns and dead ends and has been known to be quite uncomfortable at times. It also has the potential to bring you happiness, peace of mind, joy, fulfillment, freedom, meaning, and enlightenment." (Gershon & Straub, 1989).

Like the first step in all 12-step programs, the trip home calls upon us to finally surrender our self-defeating behavior and replace it with life-generating behavior. To do so requires a road map in the form of step-by-step directions, which is the primary purpose of this section of the book. Please seriously note, these are 12 steps, not 12 'stand-stills'. They require action; the kind of action that's driven by what's been heard for years in AA meetings: "If you keep on doing what you've always done, you'll keep on getting what you've always got." With

41

a little spin these same words mean, "If you keep on doing what you've always done and expect to get different results, that's nuts!" Hence the journey Going Home calls upon us to finally challenge the conclusions and fears that long ago helped but now only keep us circling the drain. The following 12 steps are listed in a recommended order. I encourage you to do a thorough job with each one before traveling on to the next.

Step One — Identify Your Self-Defeating Behavior

It's impossible to eliminate a self-defeating behavior if you don't first of all identify it and isolate it. To assist in this process, the following checklist is provided with examples of commonly practiced self-defeating behaviors. Use the list to identify those that you want to release and eliminate. Add yours if it hasn't been included.

___**Substance Abuse**	___**Underachievement**
___**Inferiority**	___**Perfectionism**
___**Excessive Worry**	___**Indecision**
___**Alienation of Others**	___**Dependency**
___**Defensiveness**	___**Disorganization**
___**Worrying**	___**Suspiciousness**
___**Depression**	___**Procrastination**
___**Overeating**	___

As you make your selection(s), keep in mind that a self-defeating behavior is defined as any behavior or attitude that is used to such an extent that it interferes with the best life possible for you. Also keep in mind the suggestions that were offered in Part One of this book about personal feedback you've received over the years, family or environmental behavior patterns you may have modeled and the continuing signals from your internal guidance system or gyroscope about choices you've made in your life. If you're still undecided after that, you may want to consider requesting the assistance of a professional therapist or psychological coach to help you sort this out.

Even though you'll probably be able to identify a number of defeating behaviors, remember that it's more manageable to initially select just one to work on...the most serious one. By following this suggestion, many people have discovered that the less distressing behaviors they also could have chosen turned out to be part of the ripple or exhaust from the main behavior and subsequently disappeared along with it. It's a nice discovery!

Step Two—Isolate the Flashpoint Situations

It is essential to understand that self-defeating behaviors are selected for use in certain situations, locations and moments in time. They are not used twenty-four hours a day, seven days a week. Hence, an important step on the road home is to identify when, where, with whom and under what circumstances your behavior is used. The following chart is designed to log and pinpoint the specific flashpoints that prompt your use of the behavior.

Self-Defeating Behavior: _____

Where: _____

When: _____

With Whom: _____

Circumstances: _____

Self-Defeating Behavior: _____

Where: _____

When: _____

With Whom: _____

Circumstances: _____

Self-Defeating Behavior: _____

Where: _____

When: _____

With Whom: _____

Circumstances: _____

Self-Defeating Behavior: _____

Where: _____

When: _____

With Whom: _____

Circumstances: _____

I recall a story that I heard on a Ram Dass tape that nicely enhances an understanding and importance of this step. It was an initial conversation between Ram Dass and a client that went something like this:

Client: "I came to see you today because I am so depressed."
Ram Dass: "You're really depressed, huh?"
Client: "Yes, it's awful."
Ram Dass: "Are you totally depressed?"
Client: "Yes, of course, I'm totally depressed."
Ram Dass: "Is there any part of you that is not depressed?"
Client: "No, none, it's terrible!"
Ram Dass: "Is the part of you that's noticing the depression, is that part depressed too?"
........After a long and puzzled pause............
Client: "Well, when you ask it that way, I guess the answer is no."
Ram Dass: "Apparently then, part of you is not depressed."

This sequence of surgically accurate questions served to open the client's mind and let in the light. It forced him to back up far enough from his depressive behavior to witness it as something he was doing instead of a condition he was afflicted with. Buddhists call this "detached awareness". This conscious revelation then prompted a very helpful subsequent discussion of where, when, with whom, why and how he depressed himself. The insights gained were both freeing and empowering.

Step Three—Identify Your Favorite Techniques

As mentioned previously, most people believe that their self-defeating behavior just "happens" without warning or cause which thereby renders them feeling like helpless victims. Although the process of putting a self-defeating behavior into operation is admittedly rapid and illusive, when it's brought into consciousness, freeze-framed and examined closely, clear sense can be made of how the choice is actually carried out and the techniques that are used in the process. Techniques serve as implementing devices. Like gears in an assembly line or ingredients in a recipe, they insure the production of the final self-defeating product. Without them, there'd be no self-defeating behavior. Therefore, it is necessary to identify both the internal and external techniques used each time the behavior is put into operation in order to eventually be able to catch yourself using them and reverse the process. Remember, internal techniques are private thought processes whereas external techniques are visible actions. Look over the following checklists and identify your favorites.

Internal Techniques

___Dwelling upon past hurts   ___Distorting feedback

___Anticipating negative results   ___Comparing oneself to others

___Making a mountain out of a molehill   ___Denying the truth

___Creating unrealistic expectations   ___Taking things out of context

___Creating false limitations   ___Holding back honest feelings

Of all these internal techniques, I want to draw particular attention to creating unrealistic expectations. For one reason or another, it seems to be a popular technique among so many of my clients and recently I discovered that it's also one of my own favorites in a self-defeating behavior I'm trying to eliminate. Somewhere in his writings, Dr. Abraham Maslow said something like this: "People who suffer alot, often times do so because they're cognitively wrong about what they think they have a right to expect." Good stuff!

External Techniques

___Failing to meet obligations   ___Manipulating others

___Inappropriate laughing or crying   ___Analyzing instead of acting

___Arguing for the sake of argument   ___Drinking too much

___Withholding in a loving relationship ___Lying

___Gambling   ___Pouting

___Spending money you don't have   ___Being late for appointments

Step Four—Do a Thorough Damage Assessment

I can't stress enough the importance of this step. Without an honest, thorough assessment of the physical, mental, social, interpersonal, spiritual, financial, vocational, and emotional consequences of the behavior, the motivation to change will be insufficient. To get at the magnitude of these damaging results, I suggest the following simple circle exercise which my clients over many years have used with great success.

Directions:

1. Get a plain piece of paper—the bigger the better.
2. Draw a dime-size circle in the center.
3. Write the self-defeating behavior you most want to eliminate in the circle.
4. Draw four dime-size circles around the center circle and connect them to your self-defeating behavior with half-inch straight lines.
5. Fill each of the four circles with a damaging result that comes from your self-defeating behavior.
6. Then connect more dime-size circles off each of the four circles and fill them with whatever results are generated from the result in the connected circle.
7. Repeat number six until the page is filled.*

As you do this exercise, keep in mind the following categories of potential results:

---

* By the way, if the self-defeating behavior you're working on is perfectionism, try to resist the temptation to use a dime and a ruler. It's just an exercise-everything will be okay.

1. **Physical Results:** Loss of energy, psychosomatic problems, respiratory problems, digestive problems, elimination problems, skin eruptions, migraines, flushing, blushing, tension, weight problems, etc.
2. **Mental/Emotional Results:** Living in fear, discouragement, defensiveness, confusion, poor self-image, guilt, shame, etc.
3. **Social/Interpersonal Results:** Family disappointment, insensitivity, mistrust of others, alienation, poor sex life, few real friends, etc.
4. **Vocational/Educational Results:** Poor school performance, poor job performance, no employment, no advancement opportunity, etc.
5. **Financial Results:** Money lost because of the perpetuation of the defeating behavior, debt, bills, etc.
6. **Spiritual Results:** Loss of connection with God or higher power, loss of peace, loss of hope, etc.
7. **Missed opportunities:** All the life experiences and joy that could have been.

When the exercise is completed, it should look something like the brief example in Figure 7 of the self-defeating behavior of excessive drinking and its results. What starts out as a single behavior can rather quickly be seen to have far-reaching consequences.

This circle exercise is designed to dismantle the denial system and hasten the surrender of the self-defeating behavior. It's also designed to offset and render foolish the popular notion of euphoric recall whereby people selectively remember the deceiving good they associate with their self-defeating behavior instead of the real overwhelming damage.

As a word of caution, I'd like to suggest that you not be misled if a few of your circles at the conclusion of the exercise contain what appear to be positive results. For example, I once worked with a client who practiced the self-defeating behavior of perfectionism. One of the results from this behavior on her circle exercise was a job promotion because her boss liked her excessively thorough work. This single positive outcome amidst the rest of the negative ones made her question whether perfectionism was really a defeating behavior. To help sort out her confusion, I then asked her a number of questions about her work habits and discovered the following: Her job started every day at 8:00 a.m. but she was always there by 6:00 a.m. To get there by 6:00 a.m., she got up every morning at 4:00 a.m. to make certain that her hair, her make-up, her outfit and her shoes were all "perfect." She'd even stop at an all-night car wash to insure that her car was perfect, too. I then told her, "Yes, you're getting promoted but you're also courting a date with an undertaker because the human system isn't rigged up to take this abuse. You're also probably driving your colleagues and loved ones nuts. Sooner or later this perfectionism is bound to bring you down."

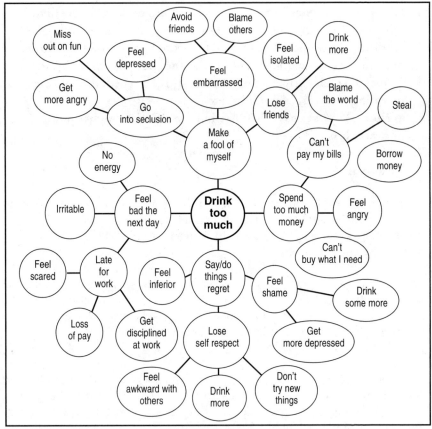

Figure 7

Returning to the one-way elevator in Figure 8, the circle exercise provides an opportunity to put a glass floor and ceiling in the elevator compartment to help us see where we've been, where we are and where we're headed in terms of consequences if the behavior isn't dropped and replaced. If assessment is done honestly so that the proverbial skunk is pulled out of the cellar (psychic cellar) and thrown on the porch, the impact should be overwhelming in favor of getting on with the long-overdue process of reclaiming our lives. If, on the other hand, the results of the damage assessment look good, something's gone awry. Either a not-so-serious SDB was chosen, or the process of denial and minimizing has already begun.

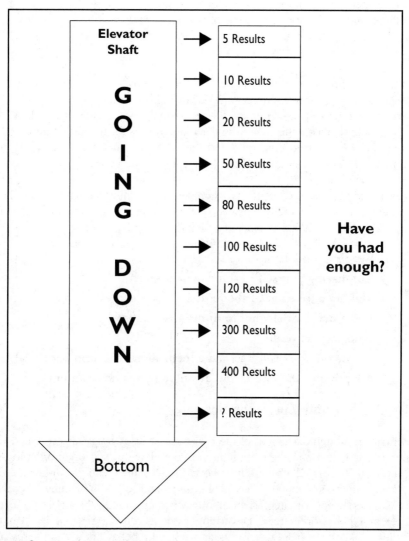

Figure 8

Step Five—Identify Your Minimizing Strategies

"Bottoming out," a popular and useful concept in the chemical dependency treatment business, can also be used for self-defeating behavior theory. It essentially means that there's a floor on the elevator where you finally get off because you're sick and tired of being sick and tired and you've had enough. It's a crucial moment in the change process for anyone wishing to say good-bye to their self-defeating behavior. It's a time of surrender and recognition that their old friend has actually been betraying them for a long time and that, in spite of the perfume, the pig still stinks.

Were it not for our creative and magnificent talent at minimizing and denying the far-reaching consequences from our self-defeating behaviors, our bottoms would be identified sooner and we'd get off the elevator on a higher floor. But minimizing disallows the use of the damaging results for instructional purposes. Hence, the lessons go unlearned and the bill to our mind and our body gets more costly as the elevator and our lives continue down the shaft.

The following checklist contains examples of the most common minimizing strategies. Use it to identify whatever you do to reduce the severity of the current and projected damage from your self-defeating behavior.

___**Keeping too busy to face the results**

___**Comparing yourself to someone worse off**

___**Making a joke out of the results**

___**Using drugs or alcohol to numb the results**

___**Ignoring the results**

___**Distorting the results to make them somehow seem beneficial**

___**Adapting to the results and arranging your life around them**

Step Six—Identify Your Disowning Targets

A rather thorough discussion of the dynamics of disowning was presented earlier in Part Two. It may be helpful for you to review that section in order to proceed with Step Six which calls upon you to specifically identify your favorite disowning targets. Remember, disowning is a mental process of blaming other people, things, events or circumstances in order to explain, justify or excuse a self-defeating behavior pattern. Disowning is dangerous because it leads us to believe that we're helpless victims and that our behaviors and attitudes are, therefore, out of our own control. Through disowning, we abandon our capacity to make life-generating choices as well as our ability to escape from the defeating behavior cycle.

The following checklist contains a few examples of frequently used disowning targets. Add yours if it hasn't been included.

___My upbringing	___The cop
___My parents	___My children
___My teacher	___My spouse
___My boss	___My emotions
___My mind	___My job
___My body parts	___My neighbor(s)
___My genes	___My temper
___My self-discipline	___The government
___My horoscope	___God
___The weather	___The Devil
___Alcohol	___My DNA
___Drugs	___
___Our society	___
___The church	___
___The bartender	___
___The judge	___

If you continue to place the responsibility for your defeating behavior pattern on any of these targets, then you simply can't own the behavior. And, if you don't own your behavior, there's no way you can do anything about it. You'll stay stuck and helpless and, more than likely, you'll eventually create additional targets to blame.

Typically, the concept of disowning is rather easy to understand and most people are able to successfully use the check list. What's far more complicated to comprehend is that the actual underlying purpose of the disowning process is to provide a subtle yet acceptable means to keep our self-defeating behavior going. If you'll recall the battle of the two forces, the conscious force to get rid of our self-defeating behavior (Force I) was driven by the weight of its damaging consequences. The unconscious force to retain our self-defeating behavior was propelled by the ancient and phony conclusion and mythical fears which claim the behavior is still necessary for psychic safety (Force II). Disowning, in a weird sort of way, allows us to ride the fence between both forces. It enables us to strongly agree with Force I and the need to dump the behavior while at the same time claiming helplessness to do anything about it which thereby allows Force II to dominate. Consequently, through the process of disowning, the behavior continues, the damage mounts and our estrangement from our psychic and spiritual home grows stronger.

Step Seven—Identify A Replacement Behavior

The seventh step in the process of going home requires the identification of a life-generating behavior to replace the departing defeating behavior. Without such a replacement, the conscious mind is forced to contend with a vacuum which then increases the likelihood of relapse to the old and familiar pattern. If you've ever had the experience of a tooth extraction, you'll recall the memory of your tongue exploring the hole for the next few days trying to help you adjust and make sense out of what's happened to your mouth. In a similar sense, saying goodbye to a long-standing self-defeating behavior creates a void and feelings of being incomplete and uncertain as to how to proceed.

Inherent in the Theory of Eliminating Self-Defeating Behaviors is the cornerstone belief that each one of us has a healthy inner self that's capable of making life-generating choices. This inner self was abandoned when we took on our self-defeating behavior in response to the toxic encounters from our environment. Now, after painfully acknowledging that our self-defeating behavior has actually betrayed us, it's time to pull our best self off the shelf and once again honor its wisdom through the signals it sends from our internal guidance system.

Life-generating behaviors are healthy alternatives to self-defeating behaviors. Instead of creating misery, they generate life-affirming results which we can then use to nourish ourselves for further growth. Instead of being driven by a phony conclusion and mythical set of fears, they are motivated by the very real fears associated with the accumulated and projected damage from our self-defeating behavior. Life-generating behaviors are, therefore, smart because they have our genuine best interest in mind. And, since they are natural responses from our integrated self, they're less complicated and much easier to use. Just as self-defeating behaviors yield self-defeating results, life-generating behaviors yield life-generating results which are then stored in our unconscious mind as reinforcement and encouragement for further use of the behavior.

To identify a life-generating replacement behavior, the following questions are offered as a guide:

1. What are the available choices you could be using in place of the self-defeating behavior you have been using? In other words, every time you opt to go with your self-defeating behavior out of the mistaken belief that you'll be better off, what healthy alternative choices could you be making?

2. Look deeply inside yourself and listen to the signals and wisdom that beep from your internal guidance system. Take an honest personal inventory of your skills, abilities, talents, instincts, strengths and resources. Which of these, either individually or in combination, could you be relying upon for assistance in the situations where you currently use your self-defeating behavior?

3. What life-generating behaviors are you currently using in the many situations and circumstances where you don't defeat yourself? Are any of these behaviors possible alternatives to your self-defeating behavior?

4. When other people are successful in the same flashpoint situations where you routinely defeat yourself, what life-generating choices do you suppose they're making to earn their healthy results?

Answers to these questions are likely to reveal that you've been robbing yourself of a full-service bank of choices at your command for use in situations where you've consistently relied upon a behavior that produces the exact opposite of what you most want. Some of these choices may be included on the following checklist. If not, spaces are provided for your additions to the list. Remember to choose just one to start and that it must be specific to best fit your situation.

<u>Examples of Life-Generating Choices</u>
___Develop clear goals and strive toward them
___Make and keep commitments
___Manage everyday affairs
___Forgive and forget past troubles
___Learn from past mistakes
___Make new friends
___Work toward maintaining friendships
___Strive for life balance

___Work on being objective and realistic
___Develop spiritual growth and activities
___Search for knowledge
___Develop sobriety and serenity
___Develop more humility
___Practice more patience
___Develop more empathy
___Become more assertive when appropriate
___Strive for fairness
___Create more self-discipline
___Stay open to life on life's terms
___Practice wellness behaviors (diet and exercise)

Step Eight—Identify Replacement Techniques

Assuming that you were successful with Step Seven in identifying a life-generating replacement behavior, the next step is to make it work. A life-generating behavior doesn't just happen because you've checked the list. It too, like a self-defeating behavior, requires a methodology to carry it out. One of my friends, an accomplished philosopher and artist periodically says, "You can pray for potatoes all day long but eventually you've got to pick up a hoe." Another dear friend says "If the only tool you have in your toolbox is a hammer, then every problem starts to look like a nail." Life-generating techniques are the necessary tools to get the job done. Without them, the replacement behavior falls apart and the risk of relapse to the old self-defeating behavior pattern increases.

Life-generating techniques are any kind of thought or action that help promote and deliver the desired life-generating outcome. They can be privately internal or visibly external. Internal techniques are private thought processes such as learning from past mistakes, anticipating positive outcomes and creating appropriate expectations. External techniques are observable actions that assist in the implementation of the replacement behavior.

Techniques must be tailored and matched to the particular behavior they're implementing. If, for example, you're trying to eliminate the self-defeating behavior of procrastination and replace it with the life-generating alternative of taking timely action, a different set of techniques will be required than if you're trying to replace excessive worry. In other words, one size doesn't fit all. Different tools will be required for different jobs. Consequently, it's not possible to provide you with a checklist of commonly used replacement techniques because they have to be individually crafted to the desired replacement behavior and outcome.

The illustration in Figure 9 is designed to map the operational process involved in replacing the self-defeating behavior of problem drinking with the healthy alternative choice of sobriety. The motivation for the selection of sobriety is driven by the very real (not mythical) fears associated with the accelerating negative consequences of continued drinking (Figure 7).

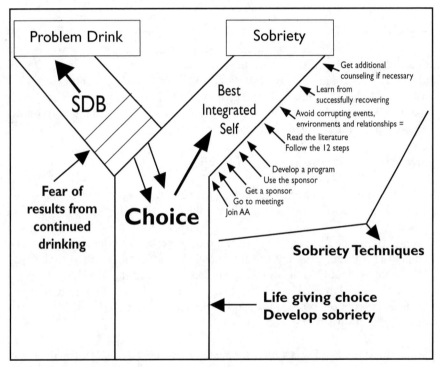

Figure 9

To help carry out and deliver the desired outcome, the following techniques are required. Without them, the choice of sobriety may regretfully turn out to be a failed intention instead of a life-affirming outcome.

1. Join A.A.
2. Go to meetings

3. Get a sponsor
4. Use the sponsor
5. Develop a program
6. Follow the 12 Steps
7. Read the literature
8. Avoid corrupting events, environments and relationships
9. Learn from successfully recovering people
10. Get additional counseling if required

I suggest that you develop your own personal replacement techniques by writing down the thoughts and actions that will be required to accomplish your life-generating replacement behavior. If, for example, your choice is to become more physically healthy, what techniques will be required to get there? If your choice is to become more organized and efficient, what tools will be required for the task? Keep in mind that the identification of life-generating techniques is not a tricky clinical issue. Rather, it's a practical matter of defining and following a course of action with your eye on the goal.

Step Nine—Seize the Moment of Choice

A few years ago I was in a cafeteria line sliding my tray along and making selections for my lunch. As I progressed down the line, I was fascinated by the man immediately in front of me who quite obviously hadn't missed many meals in his life. He seemed to grab every item the cafeteria had to offer and by the time he got to the cashier, his tray was heaping with food. As he reached for his wallet, I watched him look at his tray, pause and then exclaim aloud to himself in disbelief, "God, I'm not even hungry! Look at all this food!" With a big smile on his face, he then put most of the food back, apologized to the cashier and went off to enjoy his salad and iced tea.

What I had witnessed was a man seizing the moment of choice by catching himself in the process of implementing his self-defeating behavior and then reversing it. It was a moment of empowerment facilitated by his conscious mind and internal gyroscope telling him that a better choice was available than the loaded tray. It was also a moment of joy because the choice he ultimately made at the cash register disallowed the addition of more painful results to the pile already accumulated from his self-defeating behavior. It was a clear indication of movement from the nighttime, fog and dusk of his mind into the conscious light of day. It was a benchmark to remember the next time another moment to make a healthy eating choice came his way.

Experiences like this are common on the trip home. They're also to be expected and necessary because the change process is much more than a matter of flipping switches. It requires a conscious effort to repeatedly catch ourselves as we again and again initiate our self-defeating behavior through favorite techniques in flashpoint situations.

The awareness gained from our experiences of seizing the choice moment provides the opportunity to reverse the process and make use of the life-generating choices and techniques identified in Steps Seven and Eight. It also serves as a prevention device by helping us get ahead of our defeating pattern instead of being dragged along behind it. In other words, the more sensitive we become to our particular flashpoint situations, defeating choices, techniques and replacement behaviors, the more likely we'll be able to stop and reverse the pattern. Remember, if you don't create it, you don't have to eliminate it.

Step Nine requires attentiveness and patience as well as an expectation that the process for awhile will be one of zig-zagging between the old and the new. Saying good-bye to old familiar methods of operating and hello to new ones can sometimes feel like being on a tennis court with golf shoes. However, with conscious effort and practice, the new choices and techniques and their corresponding life-affirming results eventually become natural and reinforcing.

Step Ten—Identify Life Generating Results

Each success at seizing the choice moment and implementing a healthy replacement behavior will be followed by life-generating results which, in turn, will produce even further results. The purpose of Step 10 is to collect and record these results so that they can be used to reinforce further use of the behavior. The circle exercise utilized for the damage assessment in Step Four can also be used in Step Ten. The directions are essentially the same except that the beginning circle contains a life-generating behavior (identified in Step Seven) in place of the original self-defeating behavior. The subsequent circles in the exercise are then filled with the many positive consequences that ripple from the replacement behavior in the center circle.

The example illustration in Figure 10 presents a partial display of likely outcomes from the life-generating choice of sobriety which was previously implemented in Step Eight, Figure 9 as a replacement to the self-defeating behavior of problem drinking. When these life-affirming outcomes are compared with the damage assessment results in Figure 7, five rather conspicuous observations can be made:

1. **Both sets of results are contagious; they spread and multiply.**

2. **Self-defeating results predictably create more grief.**

3. **Life-generating results predictably create more life and joy.**

4. **Both sets of results refute the original claim of the psychic conclusion and fears about the necessity of the self-defeating behavior for psychic safety.**

5. **Both sets of results expose the psychic conclusion and fears to be what they actually are—phony and mythical**

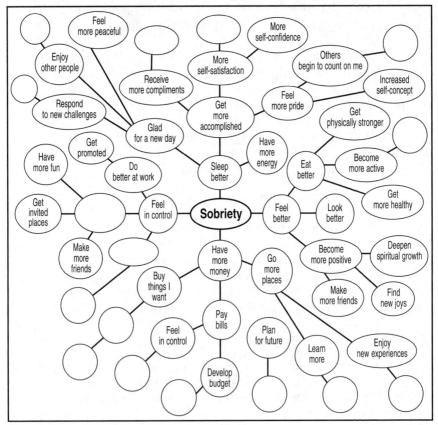

Figure 10

The illustration in Figure 11 is simply designed to outline the choice/outcome process. If both of the circle exercise assessments are done honestly and thoroughly, it becomes obvious that there's only one choice to get home.

Step Eleven—Maximize and Enjoy the Results

This is a simple yet very important step. It requests that you give yourself permission to now enjoy and maximize the healthy results you've earned through your life-generating choices. It calls upon you to use the results as energy and encouragement toward new ventures, endeavors and learnings about yourself and your world. Don't reduce these results or dismiss whatever honest compliments, praise or feedback may come your way because of them. Take deserved credit and build upon your successes. It further reinforces the new behavior and helps the integration of this life generating behavior within your self-concept.

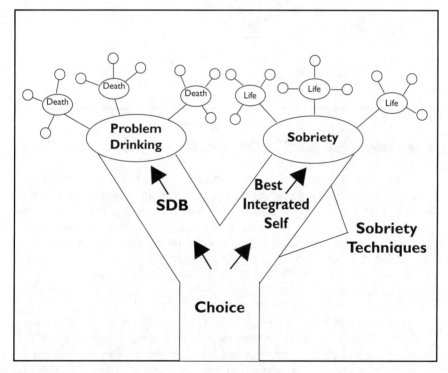

Figure 11

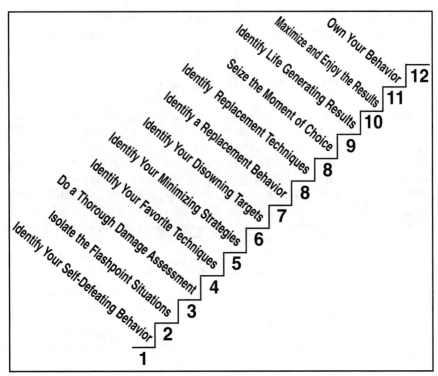

Figure 11

Step Twelve - Own Your New Behavior

The final step on the journey home is to fully recognize and accept that the rediscovery and recovery of excitement, joy, peacefulness and purpose is not a fluke. Rather, it is the direct result of your new choices. To get to Step Twelve, you had to own your defeating behavior pattern and then put considerable time, thought and energy into replacing it. Whereas the elevator brought you down, you had to climb the steps (Figure 12) to get back up. Since you climbed them, the credit belongs to you.

Figure 12

Ownership brings with it a feeling of healthy empowerment over choices and outcomes. Without it, responsibility for the continuing direction of our lives becomes the sole product of fate or luck which, in turn, renders us helpless and vulnerable to once again being controlled by new or former self-defeating behaviors.

Honest effort and adherence toward the completion of the preceding 12 Steps will be sufficient for most people to successfully eliminate their self-defeating behavior. Those who find it otherwise may need to delve more thoroughly into the historical why of their behavior which will involve a closer examination of the psychic conclusion and fears which, you'll recall, were developed at a time in our lives when we were particularly vulnerable to toxic input from our environment. As we stumbled (back then) with success upon the unconscious discovery of a behavior that relieved our distress, worry, terror, loneliness, etc., we latched onto it as a very dear friend and concluded that it was thereafter necessary for emotional insurance and security. This psychic conclusion subsequently became a description of what we expected our new behavior to prevent, i.e., withdrawal and inferiority will prevent further hurt and pain; perfectionism will prevent rejection by others; procrastination will prevent our best efforts from being judged poorly, etc. As these psychic conclusions took hold, corresponding fears developed about what we could expect if we didn't keep using our new behavior, i.e., if I don't continue to practice inferiority, then I will get hurt; if I don't continue to practice perfectionism, then I will get rejected; if I don't continue to drink alcohol, then I won't have any confidence; etc. Initially, these conclusions and fears made good emotional sense. Like hand-in-glove, they meshed together to motivate the continuation of the behavior. In fact, the stronger the conclusion and fears combination, the more dangerous it became to rely upon anything but the behavior. Consequently, as time went by, our most healthy inner choices and attitudes for responding to life's new moments and situations became shelved and ignored.

The continuation of our self-defeating behavior is prompted by an unconscious and ongoing trust and belief in the conclusion and fears. As long as that trust exists, the behavior will be seen as essential to offset psychic vulnerability. In her struggle to eliminate the self-defeating behavior of excessive worry and replace it with responsible planning, one of my clients said, "I can't believe that worrying doesn't do any good; The things I worry about never happen." This convoluted thinking is a typical example of the 'fall-out' from emotional attachment to the combination of a phony conclusion and corresponding mythical fears. It says, "Worrying is necessary and without it, I'm in trouble." It deceives the owner into believing that excessive worry is responsible for successful outcomes and happy endings. At the same time, it belies the long-standing monumental damage that the behavior actually produced which resulted in her request and need for therapy.

If the 12 Steps aren't enough to break the cycle of self-defeat, it may now be necessary to accurately test the validity of both the conclusion and fears to determine if they're delivering the promise they claim. The following three questions should do the job:

1. **What emotional vulnerability and damage is your behavior supposed to prevent?**
2. **What do you fear will be the outcome if your behavior isn't used?**
3. **What is the actual outcome when you use your behavior?**

This three-question test is designed to say, "Surrender your behavior because it's not living up to its promise. In fact, it's consistently delivering the very opposite of what you expected." For example, when the problem drinker takes this test, the following discoveries are routinely made:

- **I drank to make friends and ended up making enemies.**
- **I drank for self-confidence and ended up full of doubt.**
- **I drank to be cool and ended up a fool.**
- **I drank to be sociable and ended up in fights.**
- **I drank to feel free and ended up in jail.**
- **I drank to be more sexual and ended up impotent.**
- **I drank to relax and ended up exhausted.**
- **I drank to forget problems and ended up with more.**
- **I drank to cope with life and ended up in despair.**

When the outcome from this simple test is used in conjunction with the results from the circle exercises in Steps Four and Ten, faith in the phony conclusion and mythical fears becomes replaced with a new willingness to trust our deeper selves and greet life with fresh attitudes and choices.

Man Overboard
Part III

...The man who had been thrown overboard sat in a bed of rocks on the bottom of the ocean, his arms wrapped tightly around the anchor which he believed had saved his life. He knew he could not hold his breath much longer; his chest ached, and his head felt as if it would explode. Finally, he gave in. He let out his breath in a great burst and, when he did, his mouth filled with sea water. He tried to swallow, but the salty fluid seeped down his throat and into his lungs. He coughed violently. He knew he was drowning.

He looked to the anchor that had been his salvation. Somewhat tentatively, he loosened his hold on the iron shaft and felt his body float away. "Maybe if I let go completely," he thought. "It might not help, but I am going to die anyway."

Nearing unconsciousness, the man saw that his only hope was to let go of the anchor. He relaxed his arms and let them float free. At that moment, his body began to rise up from the floor of the ocean. He felt himself being carried upward by the water. Above him he saw a light, which grew brighter as he continued to float upward. He used his arms to push himself toward the brightness; he knew now that he might survive. With a burst of energy, he thrust his arms downward and, as he did, his face broke the surface of the water. He drew in a great breath of brisk sea air. As his vision cleared, he saw the cruise ship from which he had fallen and, on its deck, a party of anxious rescuers. And all around him, the light of the sun; directly overhead in all its brightness shone the sun.

PART FOUR

Assessment and Applications

PSYCHIC GARDENING

.......each day is a journey and the journey itself is home. – Basho

LGB:

HOPEFULLY WE HAVE made it clear that the process of "Going Home" is never finished and we are always walking on the path of imperfection. The goal is never perfection, but rather making choices that promote the best of who we are and who we can become. Psychic gardening is offered as a supplementary tool to assist on the road going home. Initially conceived by Milton Cudney in the 1970s as a self assessment tool to assist counseling, it was since further developed by Gregory Boothroyd, who has introduced psychic gardening for the past several years to counselors in training as well as at workshops for a variety of mental health professionals across the country. Most recently, I have taught the tool to my clients and also provided it in telecourse format as a tool for psychological and spiritual growth.

Part of the beauty of psychic gardening is its simplicity. The process provides non-clinical and non-pathologizing language to communicate with ourselves, loved ones and clients. At the heart of psychic gardening is a message of self-care, with tools to help us identify how we may be burning ourselves out or becoming holistically depleted. Psychic gardening is a metaphor that provides a way of sharing needs with partners, friends and family. If you're interested in the latest ideas of positive psychology, this is also a way of identifying strengths and characteristic virtues, both in yourselves and your clients. I often share this exercise with my clients, whether they are coming to me for counseling/psychotherapy, or for professional coaching services.

I'd like to take you through the nuts and bolts of psychic gardening after providing a theoretical framework within the field of positive psychology and systems theory. So, put on your gardening gloves and your favorite hat – here we go!

Positive Psychology

In January of 2000, the American Psychologist published a special issue on the topic of Positive Psychology. This issue signaled an emergence of interest in the development of a science of "positive subjective experience, positive individual traits, and positive institutions", which promised to "improve quality of life and prevent the pathologies that arise when life is barren and meaningless"

(Seligman & Csikszentmihalyi, 2000, p.12). The contributing psychologists in this issue purported a gap in the knowledge base of psychological theory and predicted that this century would bring a science and practice of positive psychology which would support and build an understanding of factors that could allow "individuals, communities, and societies to flourish" (Seligman & Csikszentmihalyi, 2000, p.5).

The basic message underlying the positive psychology movement is clear: We know a great deal about pathology and the weaknesses of the human experience, but very little is known about what makes life worth living, or what constitutes happiness and positive growth. Some of the common questions posited by positive psychology include: What makes a good life? How do typical people survive and thrive under difficult conditions? How do people flourish? What encourages positive traits, such as happiness, creativity, hope, contentment, satisfaction, courage, forgiveness, and wisdom? The purpose of positive psychology is to initiate a change in the emphasis of psychology from preoccupation with repairing the worst things in life to creating and promoting positive, life-enhancing qualities. Rather than a medical model stance of repairing after the damage has been done, positive psychology values holism, wellness, and subjective experiences.

Positive psychology takes a strong stance on prevention as well. This prevention perspective also focuses on building individual strengths and competencies, rather than on correcting or rehabilitating weaknesses or mental illnesses. Is it possible to prevent problems such as school related violence, depression and schizophrenia? Prevention research has shown that human strengths can act as a buffer to prevent the development of mental illness; part of this work requires a deeper, empirical understanding and a knowledge of how to introduce and promote these virtues in people.

I'm not suggesting or purporting the process of psychic gardening to be an empirically valid assessment. Psychic gardening is a way to identify and maintain strengths and quality of life. It is a beneficial self-help tool and can easily be adapted for use with clients, students and workshop participants. The language is a helpful way to teach individuals to communicate needs and also to share their gifts with family, friends, partners, colleagues and society.

Growing life inside the self

To know how to grow life inside yourself and become an effective psychic gardener, you should first know some ideas of systems and how they are arranged; specifically we need to consider how humans fit into the 'big picture'.

Our universe is comprised of systems that lie within systems and as we move in or out from a particular system there are openings each way. Each part of this system has a "life circulatory system" consisting of life going "in" or "out". I always imagine an infinity sign as I consider this circulatory system. For example, our bodies are open to the environmental systems we live in and are also part of our internal systems. Each entity within the universe is a distinct phenomenon in and of itself – yet also part of something larger than itself.

Human consciousness is a miraculous creation and also perhaps a product of "life circulation". It is the ability to do something and at the same time stand back and witness what we are doing. We are able to use our consciousness to do for ourselves what the systems we live within do for us – create and nurture a nourishing array of 'life foods' that grow within our psychic soil. Each of us are also systems, individuals with consciousness and the ability to make choices that are either, ultimately, self-defeating or life-generating. By bringing awareness to the ability to bring life into ourselves, nurture it as a gardener tending to seeds and plants, we can send life out to others as well. We can nurture our strengths and virtues in this way. This is psychic gardening at its essence. This process feels for many as if it has a psychospiritual piece to it as well, because we are exchanging life energy with something larger than ourselves. During a teleconference workshop I taught on psychic gardening, one participant commented "this feels like another way I can communicate with God."

The Path Through Your Inner Garden

It's time to take inventory of your psychic garden, the one growing inside. Whether you cultivate it or not, something is growing. Where are the weeds? Where are the roses and veggies? Are you growing any nourishing food for your psychic systems? Are you stingy with the food you do possess? Serve yourself a heaping plate of honesty and compassion as you guide yourself through the following psychic gardening steps.

1. Identify current sources of life generating energy (psychic food)

List specific examples of psychic food that's available to you in your every day life with which you do a good job of nourishing yourself. This is an opportunity to evaluate your 'self-care plan' and also just to acknowledge your current strengths. Give yourself some compliments! This list should help you get started:

Love/friendship from other people
Music
Nature
Humor
Spiritual practice
Exercise
Considering different perspectives
Human touch
Accepting praise
Taking criticism constructively
Thriving in a difficult situation
Sharing your life with children
Reading books
Traveling
Partaking in cultural events
Taking classes/workshops
Embracing the unexpected
Showing courage
Being compassionate with yourself

What would your list include? The possibilities are probably endless!

2. Identify potential sources of nourishing psychic food available to you right now.

List sources of life energy you could use to nourish your psychic gardening which you are not utilizing at the present time. Use the list from step one to jump-start your thinking. Keep in mind that this list will provide an area for you to improve upon immediately, simply by identifying them to yourself.

This process can be particularly helpful when undergoing a major life transition, like getting married or retiring. Reminding yourself of the resources you have available to nourish yourself everyday makes undergoing major change more fulfilling and less difficult.

In addition to creating a list, sometimes it is also helpful within this step to recall incidents in which you consciously were able to take nourishing energy into yourself. If you can think of moments when you have done this, write them down along with your list. I can think of simple moments, like when I accepted a hug of consolation from a dear friend, went for a run on nature trails, or just watched a spider build her web; each of these moments were opportunities in which I chose to take in nourishing life energy (psychic food). It's like planting the best seeds life has to offer in the soil banks of our psychic garden.

If you have difficulty in identifying sources and experiences of psychic nourishment, it is possible that you are at risk of neglecting your inner garden, which inevitably leads to suffering and psychic pain. Are you a helper and a giver to the point of holistic depletion? When you have an opportunity to nurture yourself are you at a loss of what to do? Grab your hoe because you have some extra tilling of your psychic soil to work on. Untended soil will still grow weeds which, unfortunately, is also the perfect environment for self-defeating behaviors to grow and thrive.

3. Identify examples of sharing and delivering nourishing life food to others.

To this point, the exercise asks us to consider the kind of psychic food we take in from the outside world and then share and deliver to others. Sometimes it helps to think of this as the fruit we have in our fruit cellars which we share openly with our neighbors. Here are some examples; please add your own:

Expression of feelings
Ideas
Humor
Listening
Talents
Skills
Giving compliments
Being honest
Sharing vulnerabilities
Admitting when we're wrong
Apologies
Expressing trust
Eagerness to learn
Good judgment
Constructive criticism
Intuition
Sharing stories
Being cooperative

Tenderness
Being spontaneous
Assertiveness
Sensitivity
Empathy

4. Identify your inner "Ebenezer Scrooge"

Using the list from step three as a springboard, acknowledge the gifts and energy (psychic food) which you possess but do not readily share with others. Where does the stinginess come from? It may be from some weeds that need to be gently, yet firmly removed from your garden. Sharing our gifts is part of every spiritual tradition and 12 step recovery program. AA reminds us that in order to keep what we have we must "give it away". St. Francis of Assisi shares in his prayer "It is in giving that we do receive". The following story always moves people and I'd like to share it with you here. It is a poem written by James Patrick Kinney from the magazine "Liguorian" and is titled "The Cold Within":

Six humans trapped by happenstance
in dark and bitter cold
Each one possessed a stick of wood
or so the story's told.

Their dying fire in need of logs
one woman held hers back
For on the faces around the fire
she noticed one was black.

The next one looking across the way
saw one not of his church
And couldn't bring himself to give
the fire his stick of birch.

The third one sat in tattered clothes
and gave his coat a hitch –
"Why should my log be used
to aid the idle rich?"

The rich man just sat back and thought
of the wealth he had in store
And how to keep what he had earned
from the lazy, shiftless poor.

The black man's face bespoke revenge
as the fire passed from his sight
For all he saw in his stick of wood
was a chance to spite the white.

The last man in this forlorn group
did not except for gain
Giving only to those who gave
was how he played the game.

Six logs held tight in death's still hands
was proof of human sin
They didn't die from the cold without
They died from the cold within.

Along with this "stinginess" inventory, list an example of a time when you did not share in proportion to what you possess. I acknowledge that I have become stingy with my time in recent years. When I started to consider it as a gift that could be shared with others, I knew it was necessary to cultivate and be more generous with my time. Strangely enough (really, there is no mystery), when I do this, it benefits me as well! It's yet another cosmic reminder of the life circulatory system.

5. Identify synchronous experiences of the life circulatory system.
We can only choose to increase optimal life experiences if we are conscious of them. Take a moment to reflect on experiences in your life when it felt as though the flow of life energy (psychic food) was being taken in and also shared outward in a balanced, reciprocal process. This kind of life exchange can feel almost transcendental, when we lose our sense of time and are totally engrossed. Positive Psychologists sometimes refer to this as the "flow" experience which was introduced by Mihayi Csikszentmihalyi (1990). Some examples might be:

A friendship that feels mutually nourishing and supportive
A marriage/partnership
Engaging in teaching – when teacher is excited and students are responsive
Sharing something and feeling understood and appreciated
Nurturing plants, which then return life
Preparing a meal for guests
Effective helping relationship (therapy, coaching)

Being comforted and comforting others during grief and loss
Sharing a talent and being applauded
Feeling connected with a higher power or something larger than yourself
Time spent caring for pets
Having fun with a child, or teaching them something important

What are the moments in your life when you experienced a higher truth, flow, reciprocity? How can you cultivate more of those moments?

6. Identify what is growing in your psychic garden as a result of your intake and sharing of psychic nourishment.

What qualities, strengths, characteristics and emotional states comprise the constellation of your life and your inner garden? What do you feel deeply attached to? Some of the positive outcomes might be things like:

Happiness
Meaning
A sense of purpose
Connection to spirit
Loving family
Positive support system
Kindness
Love
Openness
Inner Peace
Curiosity
Wisdom
Confidence
Calm energy
Creativity
Emergence of skills/talents
Empathy
Gratitude
Compassion
Patience
Commitment
Intuition
Resilience
Courage

What are more examples of life growing inside of you that are not on this list? A client once asked me "How will I know when I get there?" I asked "Where is there?" and she thoughtfully replied, "I guess it's right here!" As we laughed I suggested that she start looking for 'symptoms of inner peace'. When we feel them, we know we're on the right track.

Now what?

It seems that insight alone is much like chinese food: It tastes yummy but within a hour or so you're hungry again! This is a tool for awareness but also for growth. Commit to this process and journal or find a fellow "gardener" to talk to on a regular basis. Change is a gradual process for us and it is not a one-way street. Insight and change comes slowly, but with it also comes healing, the return of joy, authentic happiness, meaning and endless possibility.

Are any of you gardeners? I mean, literally gardeners. This past spring I became an "outer" gardener for the first time. I felt excitement as I prepared the soil and planted seedlings and young perennials with my Mom's guidance. I arranged blossoming annual flowers in large pots. Throughout May and into June I watered and nurtured my garden carefully. By July the process of weeding was growing old; I learned that even weeds have their seasons and if I ignored them, they would only go to seed, strengthen their root systems and be back again next year. There were times when my frustration resulted in neglect of the garden. Then my intended blossoms and plants began to rebel; I realized that some herbs, for example, can spread like weeds and smother out daisies and marigolds. I had to prune and balance even the intended growth. Sometimes I neglected to pick flowers and share them with others. Let's just say it was a process. By late summer, my garden became a place for me to slow down, attend, accept and appreciate. It is beautiful in its imperfections. It will never look like the pictures in a magazine and for that I am truly grateful.

My initial reactivity and subsequent acceptance and appreciation for my garden became an outer reflection of what goes on as I "inner" garden. I weed unwanted behaviors from my life in much the way I worked in the dirt this summer – steadily but not frenzied, compassionately but not apathetically. The work is never done. When I am aware of a self-defeating behavior popping back up in my psychic garden, I gently notice, pluck it and remove it, concluding that it is unworthy of living in my garden and entirely useless for the person I aspire to be. I always hope the behavior will not return as I focus on filling my garden with life-generating flora. Yet, sometimes the behavior sprouts again; so once again I pull it up until the last bit of root is removed. This process can take many seasons. That's okay! As long as we are attending in an intentional way with a mindful and gentle stance, we will bring compassion to the weeds we destroy as well as the flowers we fertilize. We have a lifetime to cultivate the inner garden that makes us each unique, vulnerable and beautiful.

"..........And then - the day came when the risk to remain tight in a bud was more painful than the risk it took to BLOSSOM!" - Anain Nin

RELATIONAL DEFEATING BEHAVIOR

"Sometimes our light goes out but it is blown again into flame by an encounter with another human being. Each of us owes deepest thanks to those who have rekindled this inner light."
- Albert Schweitzer

Introduction
LGB:

RELATIONSHIPS PROVIDE US with love, hope, laughter and light. Just as we tend to our inner garden, we also have shared soil which we tend with the fellow gardeners in our lives, those who are near and dear to us.

So far, our book has focused primarily on the individual working toward eliminating self defeating behaviors so that we may practice more life generating ones. Just as individuals practice self-defeating behaviors (often without intrapersonal awareness), so too do relationships manifest self-defeating qualities. Even the healthiest of relationships often still fall prey to the practice of self-defeating behaviors. When these behaviors are examined through the lens of the self-defeating behavior theory, we can bring relational difficulties into the light, thereby growing both as individuals as well as in relationship.

What are relational defeating behaviors?
In the spirit of the book, I'd like to continue to avoid clinical quagmires and simply propose that a relational defeating behavior is any behavior or attitude used by people within a relationship (friendship, familial, romantic) that undermines the relationship's value and meaning, thereby diminishing the best life possible for both individuals as well as the life of the relationship.

Given this definition, there are some very common relational defeating behaviors that come to mind such as:

Dishonesty
Defensiveness
Avoidance
Selfishness
Distrust/suspicion
Guilt
Victimizing
Toughness or invulnerability

Arrogance
The need to be right
Dominating
Disloyalty
Impatience
Apathy
Competitiveness
Ineffective communication
Insults/petty criticisms
Enmeshment/dependency
Irresponsibility

These behaviors are defeating because they work against the relationship's best integrated self, making it more difficult for the relationship to actualize and become a place for joy, growth and healing. Consequently, the relationship suffers as do the individuals in it.

Why and how are relational defeating behaviors perpetuated?
Relational defeating behaviors are driven by underlying irrational conclusions and fears that when combined, perpetuate patterns that can eventually destroy relationships. Just as Greg described in the chapters on individual self-defeating behaviors, together we create false conclusions and fears about our relationship in an attempt to protect ourselves from psychic pain. It seems like a helpful and safe thing to do, but it only creates more pain and suffering.

Examples of Relational Conclusion/Fear Combinations:

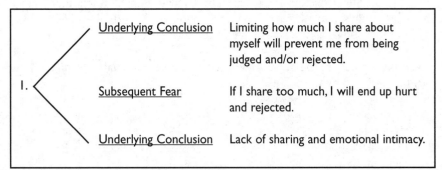

	Underlying Conclusion	Limiting how much I share about myself will prevent me from being judged and/or rejected.
I.	Subsequent Fear	If I share too much, I will end up hurt and rejected.
	Underlying Conclusion	Lack of sharing and emotional intimacy.

How are relational defeating patterns implemented?
The development of relational defeating behavior patterns in a friendship or partnership requires more than false conclusions and fears that result in the

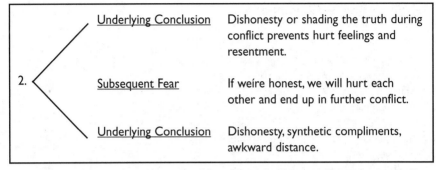

	Underlying Conclusion	Dishonesty or shading the truth during conflict prevents hurt feelings and resentment.
2.	Subsequent Fear	If we're honest, we will hurt each other and end up in further conflict.
	Underlying Conclusion	Dishonesty, synthetic compliments, awkward distance.

pulling of a 'defeat-switch'. There must also be techniques utilized which allow us to manifest the relational defeat and make the self defeating behavior come to life.

Relational Techniques (Examples)
 Remaining too busy to spend time together
 Keeping topics and activities shallow
 Using humor inappropriately
 Involving other friends or family as distractions
 Picking arguments
 Allowing frustration to remain unexpressed
 Blaming oneself completely for relational difficulties
 Blaming the other person completely for relational difficulties
 Engaging in irresponsible/unhealthy behaviors (any other individual SDB)
 Silence/refusal to engage
 Withholding emotional intimacy
 Withholding sexual intimacy
 Numerous other sabotaging techniques (we each have our favorites)

What are the results of relational defeating behaviors?
The consequences of relational defeating behaviors are painful and often devastating. They diminish the quality and potential of the relationship and create pointless suffering. Defeating results, over time, will wear down friends and partners until their hopes for a healthy and growth-promoting relationship are destroyed. Thoughts of future growth and satisfaction are abandoned. Eventually, we end the friendship, partnership or marriage and look for other possibilities (which we unfortunately often use to unconsciously create the same relational defeating behavior). The other choice we frequently make is to stay in the unsatisfying relationship and grow indifferent, distant and stagnant. Either way, we continue to create psychic pain for ourselves and those with whom we are paired.

Relational Results (Examples)

Arguments
Divorce
Ending of friendship
Psychological games (guilt trips)
Manipulation
Intimidation
Isolation
Inability to form healthy new relationships
No friends
Wishing to have a partner but remaining single
Substance abuse
Codependency

Minimizing relational defeating results

If the individuals in a relationship would listen to the best wisdom and integrated self of the relationship, they would make the difficulties instructional and healing. By doing so, they would snuff out the voice of the phony fears and conclusions. This is what makes relationships powerful and meaningful. We are always going to make mistakes and be imperfect (once again, perfection is not the goal) but why not make mistakes something we can learn from and use to heighten intimacy and connection? Unfortunately, just as we do individually, partners in relationships can create a climate of denial and refute the pain and psychic suffering. Here are some common relational minimizing strategies:

- **keep too busy to face the issues.**
- **tell ourselves (and each other) that things will somehow get better.**
- **ignore conflict.**
- **compare ourselves to other relationships that are much worse than ours.**
- **conclude that confusing conflict and painful patterns of behavior can't be avoided.**
- **focus on the wrong or less important issues.**
- **try to adapt to the pain and build our lives in an unhealthy way around them.**

Disowning relational defeating behaviors

To then complete the cycle of implementation, a relationship must now disown the defeating behavior pattern by blaming other people or circumstances. Some popular disownings include:

- **"That's how I saw my Mom and Dad argue."**
- **"I am too stressed from work"**
- **"I don't have the time/energy/patience for this right now."**
- **"This is the best I can do; this is who I am."**
- **"You're not going to listen to me even if I try to talk, so why bother?"**
- **"Maybe you just can't accept me for who I am!"**
- **"I can't help it, I have ADD/depression/bipolar/alcoholism."**

Only when we can see our individual defeating behavior patterns, own them, hold them in our conscious mind and expose them to light will we ever end the damage and pain they bring to our lives. It is the same with relational defeating patterns of behavior. We are offered a precious opportunity to learn and generate life in relationship to other people. When both individuals are committed to life generating behavior, the results are nothing short of extraordinary. But we have to first be willing to scrutinize our relationships and examine the patterns. These inquiries are critical if we are ever to understand what we do to create and maintain unsatisfying and painful relationships.

I recall a conversation I had with my Grandma many years ago. We were sitting at her kitchen table and she was patiently listening to me bemoan about my latest love relationship. I refused to take responsibility for choosing a train-wreck for a boyfriend, instead saying, "but, Grandma, I love him!" She finally looked me straight in the eye and with great compassion said, "Lori, love goes anywhere you choose to send it, even up a pig's ass." I stared at her for a minute, stunned, until both of our faces broke out into huge grins. Yes, even love is a choice and we must accept responsibility for growing it if we are ever to enjoy healthy relationships.

The continuation of individual and relational self-defeating behaviors is a dishonoring of our internal guidance system and its life-generating menu of choices. Whereas defeating behaviors predictably bring us defeating results, life-generating relational behavior creates connection and a source of life energy that gets fed back into ourselves and our partner to create growth and holistic nourishment.

81

Life Generating Relationships

A bird and a fish can fall in love, but where will they live?
– Jewish proverb

LGB:
We're conceived in attachment and exit the womb attached. Once we've become physically disattached, a never-ending longing begins for closeness, connection and reattachment. In fact, our psychic gardens would be unable to grow and flourish were it not for the inclusion and attachment of strong, healthy, loving, vulnerable people in our lives. These relationships are the plants and flowers, fruits and vegetables of our garden. As they grow, we grow. Because they nourish us, we need them and seek them out.

Unfortunately, the relational selection process is often driven by the fog, dusk or nighttime of our mind and our unions, therefore, sadly end up being guided by "when the rocks in his head fit the holes in hers." Our culture's emphasis on individuality adds to the toxicity found in relationship selection, formation and development. One of the most profound examples of cultural pathology lies in the process of gender socialization. From childhood, boys are taught to be tough, not cry, and to appear fearless. Girls are taught to be passive, self-sacrificing and emotionally restricted. As a result, our selection process and path into relationship (both heterosexual and homosexual) is inherently beset with relational defeating behaviors. We arrive at adulthood feeling incomplete without a relationship yet largely unprepared to consciously create and develop a healthy one.

Probably the most intense and profound relationships are those we share with our spouses or life partners. To enhance the success of both establishing and growing these unions, we should avoid the temptation offered through quick fixes to find the "right" partner or 'bend' the existing partner into something they are not. To do this, popular tabloid questions could be replaced with relational gardening questions.

Typical Tabloid Questions:

"How do I find Mr./Ms./Dr. Right?"

"How can we rekindle the flame we once had?"

"How do we compromise?"

"How can I become more attractive/likable/ to others?"

"Why can't I understand my spouse/partner/girlfriend/boyfriend?"

Relational Gardening Questions:

"How can I take responsibility for my SDBs so I can understand and help myself better and be more open with my partner?"

"How can I do my own psychic gardening so that I can understand better what I want and need instead of expecting my partner to figure it out?"

"Can I be the person I want to find in a partner?"

"Why do I feel scared when my partner seems to want something I don't? How can I accept differences without expecting him/her to change into what I want?"

"How can I come into relationship in a way that supports and encourages us both to find the path to 'Going Home'?"

Asking such gardening questions of ourselves opens a door to healing and growth. Relationships are powerful reflectors of who we are and lead us home if we are open to seeing the way. Our outer relationships reveal our inner relationship and if we continue to bring along the baggage of toxic garbage collected during earlier years, its poisoning impact will contaminate our selection process and then infect the growth of our relationship(s).

Qualities of Life Generating Relationships:
    Centered
    Psychically Nurturing
    Authentic
    Caring/Supportive
    Mutual/Reciprocal

Sharing common ground
Unscripted (without expectations, rigid rules, etc.)
Holistically nourishing

Life generating relationships become a safe place to share psychic wounds, bring them into light and, together, carry out a partnership of healing and intimacy. This requires the revealing of imperfections and possible vulnerability. Inevitably and fortunately, there is an almost paradoxical empowerment between people when they share vulnerability and the beautiful simplicity of imperfection. It's a relational 'superglue'........ the stuff that makes us truly whole as individuals and connected as partners.

<u>Conclusion: Going Home Together</u>

Fortunately, as many of us eventually do, I have chosen a path of healing. It's a path that includes recognizing that I will never be the perfect spouse to my husband and that I must be willing to accept responsibility for not only my gifts and strengths, but also my mistakes and flaws and use them to grow. Since Greg is also committed to the same process, it works! The bottom line is that, while on this path together, our life generating relational choices lighten the 'home-sickness' in our hearts and feed us both with spiritual and emotional energy and nourishment. As such, our journey brings us closer to home every day. I wish the same for each of you.

"When we ask ourselves which persons in our lives mean the most to us, we often find that it is those who can face the reality of powerlessness........

........and have chosen rather to share our pain, and touch our wounds with a gentle and tender hand. The friend who can be silent with us in a moment of despair or confusion, who can stay with us in an hour of grief and bereavement, who can tolerate not knowing, not curing, not healing........

........that is the friend who cares." – Henri J. Nouwen

SYSTEMIC DEFEATING BEHAVIORS

"Working around here is like being in a nightmare. I'd love to walk away from it but I need the sleep."

GB:

JUST AS INDIVIDUALS AND RELATIONSHIPS practice defeating behaviors, so too do departments, organizations, corporations, school systems and nations. When these systemic defeating behavior patterns are examined within the framework of the Self-Defeating Behavior Theory, they can be brought into consciousness, understood and eliminated.

Organizations are created by and composed of people. If the people who create or compose a particular organization, social structure, operating procedure or system practice self-defeating behaviors, then inherent in the creation or operation will be the ingredients required to maintain and perpetuate systemic defeating behaviors. Such behaviors not only work against individuals, but also against the effective operation of the organization itself.

What Are Systemic Defeating Behaviors?
Again, without getting clinically complicated, I'd like to simply suggest that a systemic defeating behavior is any behavior or attitude used by people within an organization that defeats the organization's purpose and diminishes the best life possible for its members and constituents.

Given this definition, the most common systemic defeating behaviors that I am most frequently asked to help eliminate include the following:

- Impaired Communication
- Group Dissension
- Group Cynicism
- Competing Divisions or Departments
- Group Disorganization
- Group Impotency
- Group Apathy
- Lack of Teamwork
- Group Underachievement
- Group Stagnation

- Little or No Innovation
- Rigidity of Rules
- Unnecessary Conflicts
- Group Procrastination
- Group Confusion
- Group Incompetence
- Power Struggles
- Poor Planning
- Group Withdrawal
- "Gridlock"

The reason these behaviors are defeating is that they work against the organization's best integrated self making it therefore impossible for the organization to become self-actualized. Consequently, everyone connected with the system suffers including its customers.

Examples of defeating systems abound. As a case in point, not long ago on our university campus, a moderately priced lunch restaurant opened which, given the multitude of students, had the potential of becoming a successful goldmine for its owner. When some out-of-town friends of mine unexpectedly called one morning to invite me to lunch, I suggested that we try the new restaurant because it was close to my office and I had to be back by one o'clock.

Since I had packed my lunch that day, I carried it with me into the restaurant and ordered a soft drink as my three companions ordered full lunches from the menu. To my surprise and bewilderment, my soft drink was immediately delivered to our table by the owner who promptly chastised me for bringing my lunch into the restaurant and insisted that I too order from the menu. As we left the restaurant to find another place to eat, he continued yelling about rules and regulations as if the four of us had just crawled out of a litter bag and violated the dress code of a five-star dining room. Not surprisingly, for similar ridiculousness, his restaurant closed two months later.

Shortly after that, I had another experience in a restaurant that was even more mind-boggling. I had just finished an all-day workshop and decided to get an early dinner before returning to the airport. I walked into a restaurant and told the hostess that I wanted dinner. She replied "Do you have a reservation?" I said, "No, but I'm not real hungry and I'll eat fast and be out of here." "I'm sorry, sir," was her reply, "we only serve people with reservations." I looked around her into the eating area and counted two customers and twenty-two empty tables. "Are you expecting a mob to fill these twenty-two tables in the next half hour?" I asked. "No sir, but having a reservation is one of our policies" she said politely.

I stood there for a moment thinking that I had finally discovered lunacy at a level of unparalleled proportion. And then I thought "No, this woman is just funny—a real good subtle sense of humor." So, I approached her again and said, "Look, all I want is your special tonight—whatever is the fastest." Again she replied, "I'm really sorry sir, it's just company policy."

I left the restaurant and sat in my rental car trying to make sense out of the suspended rationality of the conversation with the hostess and then, driven by indignation, I stormed back into the restaurant and told her that I wanted to make a reservation. To my everlasting disbelief she replied, "For when?" I said,

"Right now!" She said, "For how many?" I said, "One!" After writing my name down on her list, she announced, "Follow me" and led me to my table. When I finished eating, there were still twenty-one empty tables. After paying my bill, I told her to have a great day and I laughed (and scratched my head) all the way to the airport.

Another example of systemic defeating behavior I not only personally recall but have often seen duplicated in many settings concerns the process used to select and hire administrators......from department heads all the way up to chief operating officers and presidents. First comes what appears to be an automatic assumption that it is absolutely necessary to look "outside" the organization for the ideal candidate even though the best person for the position may already be right there performing wonderfully. This defeating assumption (psychic conclusion) then sets into motion a very expensive, time consuming "net-casting" process which is guaranteed to generate additional committees, additional drain on the travel and expense budget and internal group distress and resentment. Once the candidate has been located, members of the organization are then required to interrupt their work schedules and accommodate numerous sorts of "getting-to-know-you" meetings with the candidate. By everyone except those arranging them, these meetings are often seen as nothing more than synthetic gestures followed by requests for feedback which won't be listened to anyway because the decision to hire or reject the person has already been made.

In one such meeting, I recall an outside candidate who had been foisted upon us by upper administrative officers intent on "straightening" our department out. During the reciprocal question and answer period, the candidate asked the following question: "If I am offered this position, what would you want and expect from me?" In a genuinely kind manner, one of my senior colleagues promptly responded. "I believe an administrator's function is to facilitate and enable our work setting so that all of us, from secretaries to professional staff, can best do what we've been trained and hired to do. I'd want you to make sure that there's ample parking, the sidewalks are clear, the heating and air-conditioning works, the building is kept clean, the computer system functions well, necessary supplies are available, pay checks are timely, etc." Then he added, "aside from taking care of those necessary and important responsibilities along with being reasonably civil and pleasant, I'd prefer that you simply stay out of the way". My colleague was thoughtfully trying to teach the candidate that if he would do the best he could at the job of being our administrator, it would free all of us up to do the same in our own respective responsibilities. He was letting the candidate know that we're all in this together interdependently...that we all need each other. The candidate was being gently reminded what it would be like if the heart decided to work against the lungs, the liver decided to be unco-operative with the stomach, the brain decided to overthrow or do the work of the rectum, etc. A mess would surely follow! Predictably, the candidate expressed his appreciation and strong agreement with this thoughtful response to his question and then left to be paraded in front of another group for further introductions, questions and answers.

He got the job and within one month of being our new administrator was caus-ing all kinds of unnecessary trouble and conflict. The insight and direction he had solicited, supported and praised during his interview with us disappeared as he initiated power struggles, divisiveness, competition, secrecy, etc. Watching the new "boss" start to circle the drain, I remember reaching out to him with the hope of helping him save himself from himself. Gently over time, I gave him a number of questions to think about such as:

1. What do you suppose attracts people to want to work in an organization and give it their best?

2. What do you suppose keeps them there?

3. What does an organization do to help employees feel wanted or unwanted?

4. What does an organization do to create resistance in its employees?

5. What do you suppose an organization does that prompts good employees to leave?

6. Why do you suppose some organizations are so vibrant and alive while oth-ers are so dead?

7. How do you think they get that way?

I also gave him a copy of the following saying issued in the year 210 B.C.:

"We trained hard, but it seemed that every time we were beginning to form into teams we would be reorganized. I was to learn later on in life that we tend to meet any new situation by reorganizing, and what a wonderful method it can be for creating the illusion of progress while producing confusion, inefficiency, and demoralization." – Petronius Arbiter

Like trying to teach a dog to "meow", all my efforts failed. So did those of many of my other colleagues who genuinely wanted our new colleague and department to flourish. Instead, for the next thirteen years we all suffered..........personally, professionally and systemically! The psychic conclusions and fears in the mind of our new boss were so rigidly set that all he seemed able to do was intensify his defeating choices as in......'if a little bit doesn't work, more will'. The idea of 'quit digging when you're in an ever-deepening hole' simply couldn't find a pathway to his conscious mind. Eventually, like it always does, the pain, decay and destruction leaked from the departmental seams and started infesting the larger system which eventually prompted his removal and long overdue departmental and organizational relief.

Why Systemic Defeating Behaviors Are Perpetuated
Systemic defeating behaviors like these previously described are driven by underlying irrational conclusions and fears which work together, in combination, to perpetuate their existence and eventually sink the system. Like the conclusion and fears of individual self-defeating behaviors, they offer a phony promise of protection which makes the behavior then seem like a smart thing to do.

Examples of Systemic Conclusion/Fear Combinations

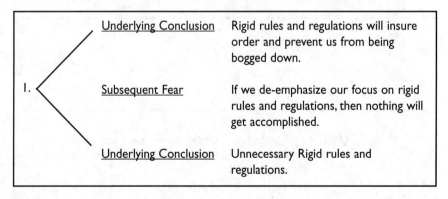

I.

Underlying Conclusion — Rigid rules and regulations will insure order and prevent us from being bogged down.

Subsequent Fear — If we de-emphasize our focus on rigid rules and regulations, then nothing will get accomplished.

Underlying Conclusion — Unnecessary Rigid rules and regulations.

2.

Underlying Conclusion	Apathy will prevent us from making poor decisions.
Subsequent Fear	If we drop our apathy, then our decisions will be criticized and rejected.
Underlying Conclusion	Group apathy.

3.

Underlying Conclusion	Disorganization will prevent anyone from taking advantage of us
Subsequent Fear	If we become organized, then too many demands will be put upon us.
Underlying Conclusion	Group disorganization.

4.

Underlying Conclusion	Underachieving will prevent our incompetence from surfacing.
Subsequent Fear	If we try our best, it woní' be good enough.
Underlying Conclusion	Group underachievement.

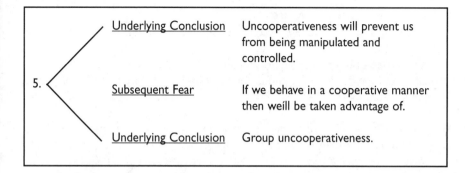

5.	Underlying Conclusion	Uncooperativeness will prevent us from being manipulated and controlled.
	Subsequent Fear	If we behave in a cooperative manner then we'll be taken advantage of.
	Underlying Conclusion	Group uncooperativeness.

How Systemic Defeating Behaviors Are Implemented

To maintain and perpetuate defeating behavior patterns within an organization requires more than retrieving phony conclusions, creating mythical fears and then throwing the self-defeat switch. Techniques must also be used like gears in an assembly line or ingredients in a recipe to actuate the behavior and guarantee its manifestation.

Systemic Techniques (Examples)

- Make operational procedures unnecessarily complicated.
- Structure the workload so that there's always a crisis to keep up with thus guaranteeing that nothing ever gets done.
- Use verbose professional jargon rather than clear simple language.
- Force employees to go underground to get stuff done.
- Focus on the wrong issues.
- Set up rules and regulations and when they're no longer appropriate, rigidly adhere to them anyway.
- Recruit, orient and promote staff who will assist in perpetuating the systemic defeating behaviors.
- Design the system so that each department fights with the other for survival thereby hurting the whole.
- Maintain program goals on paper that are unconnected with the reality of the organizational mission.
- Isolate and punish people who don't cooperate with the systemic defeating behaviors.
- Get caught up in minutia to avoid important issues.
- Give people too much to do so that they can't do anything well. Then praise them for driving themselves nuts trying to keep up.

- **Demand unnecessary reports.**
- **Create too many unnecessary committee assignments.**

Following one of my training workshops in Seattle, Washington, one of the participants sent me the following humorous and insightful story to further illustrate systemic techniques:

The tribal wisdom of the Dakota Indians, passed on from one generation to another, says that when you discover you are riding a dead horse, the best strategy is to dismount. However, in modern business, education and government, because of heavy investment costs to be taken into consideration, often other strategies need to be attempted with dead horses, including the following:

1. *Buy a stronger whip.*
2. *Try a new bit or bridle.*
3. *Change riders.*
4. *Say things like "this is the way we've always ridden this horse".*
5. *Threaten the horse with termination.*
6. *Appoint a committee to study the horse.*
7. *Arrange to visit other sites to see how they ride dead horses more efficiently.*
8. *Lower the standards so dead horses can be included.*
9. *Hire outside contractors to ride the dead horse.*
10. *Harness several dead horses together for increased speed.*
11. *Purchase an after market product to make dead horses run faster.*
12. *Form a quality focus group to find probable uses for dead horses.*
13. *Promote the dead horse to a supervisory position.*

Results of Systemic Defeating Behaviors
The consequences or results of perpetuating systemic defeating behaviors are very serious. In addition to diminishing the quality of the system's product, they extinguish the quality of life of the people working in the system. Defeating results grind away at alive people—beating them down until their hopes and dreams for a better work-life are abandoned. Eventually they either search for a more alive work setting or succumb to the organizational defeating behavior pattern and become stagnant, moldy and synthetically cooperative. Either way, the organization suffers and the behavior becomes more firmly entrenched.

Systemic Results (Examples)
- **Low production**
- **Low morale**
- **Lack of job satisfaction**
- **Waste of time, money and energy**
- **That awful feeling of not wanting to go to work**
- **Taking work dissatisfaction home to family**
- **Group dissension**
- **Group ineffectiveness**
- **Group boredom**
- **Group cynicism**
- **Truancy**
- **High employee turnover**

Figure 6 presents an illustration of the implementation cycle for the systemic defeating behavior of organizational disorganization. Six of the eight implementation ingredients are included. The remaining two, minimizing and disowning will be discussed next.

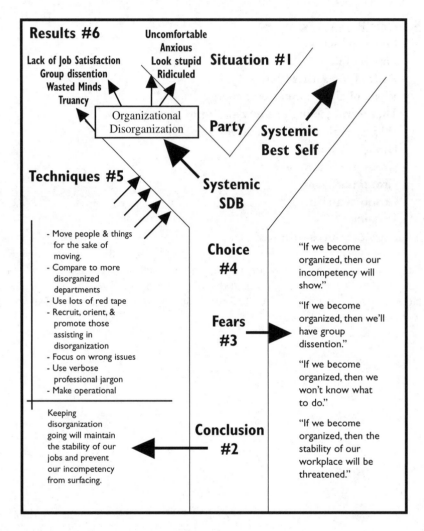

Minimizing Systemic Defeating Results

If the organization would listen to the wisdom of its best integrated self, it would make the defeating results instructional and use them to rescind the phony conclusion and mythical fears. In other words, there's no sense making mistakes if you're not going to learn from them. But, just like individuals and relationships, systems also do whatever they can to tone down, reduce or deny the pain from perpetuating systemic defeating behaviors by:

- keeping so busy that the results are ignored.

- **joking about the results.**
- **comparing the results to other departments or organizations that are worse off.**
- **perceiving the results as though they can't be avoided.**
- **adapting to the results and building a way of life around them.**

Disowning Systemic Defeating Behaviors

To complete the implementation cycle, the organization must now disown the behavioral pattern by blaming stockholders, board members, lack of time, lack of money or by using any of the following popular excuses:

- **"That's the way we've always operated."**
- **"Others do it, why shouldn't we?"**
- **"You can't change overnight."**
- **"You can't win them all."**
- **"No one will listen anyway, so why even try?"**

When our individual and relational defeating behavior patterns are owned and thoroughly examined in the conscious light of day, the consequential damage they bring to our lives will be seen as tragic. Similarly, when our systemic defeating behavior patterns are examined with the same scrutiny, the damage will be seen as monumental. Such examinations are essential if we are to figure out and reverse what we currently do to create school dropouts, drug and alcohol dependent people, child and spouse abusers, criminals, a suffering environment, etc.

The continuation of self-defeating behaviors either individually, relationally or in our organizations is a betrayal of our internal guidance system and its life-generating array of choices. Whereas defeating behaviors predictably yield defeating results, life-generating behaviors create life results which get fed back into ourselves, our relationships and our systems for nourishment and growth.

SELF-DEFEATING BEHAVIOR THEORY
AND SUBSTANCE ABUSE

An alcoholic said to a man sitting at the bar..........
"How do you do it? Every couple of days you come in here
and just have one drink."
"I don't know!" the man replied. "If I feel like it, I stop after
work. Sometimes I do and sometimes I don't. Sometimes I
just have a beer or a glass of wine, other times I just have
soda. Then I go home to my wife and kids."
"Amazing", replied the alcoholic. "If I could drink like that I
would do it all the time!"
- from 'Coyote Speaks' by Jacques Rotzky

GB:
The primary thrust of the self-defeating behavior theory is that such behaviors are things people 'do' and that there are reasons to do them, situations in which to do them, ways to do them and seriously damaging consequences for continuing to do them. Appropriately, the question often arises, "What about conditions people actually 'have' such as alcoholism and how can the theory be applied?"

As director of a university based out-patient treatment program, I've had plenty of opportunity to answer this question and link the theory with the diagnosis and treatment of substance abuse issues.......particularly those related to college student drinking. This section of the book is designed to briefly show this connection and application.

Sadly, because of both institutional and cultural denial, problem drinking continues to be characterized as a moral issue and ultimately stigmatized with the word "alcoholic". Consequently, I make a conscious effort to avoid using this word with my clients and instead talk about their relationship with alcohol, i.e., is it satisfying or self-defeating? In addition to the traditional diagnostic clinical interview and tests, I find most helpful a symptom-descriptive continuum to assist the client in plotting where they once were, where they are now and where they're heading in their relationship with alcohol.

Alcohol Relationship Continuum

Abstinence	Use	Misuse	Abuse	Dependenc
No alcohol consumption for personal, spiritual health or other reasons	Socially acceptable drinking; drink as a beverage vs. a drug; person chooses when and how much to drink.	Any use which is harmful to self or others; negative effects on schoolwork, employment, health, finances, relationships, etc.; occasional out of control drinking; pattern of drinking more than intended begins.	Planned systematic misuse of alcohol; preoccupation with partying; pattern of drinking more than intended increases; tolerance builds; blackouts begin; feel compelled to drink rather than choosing to drink; believes alcohol is required for good times.	Compelled to drink; no control once drinking beings; regularly drinks to intoxication; frequent blackouts; drinking becomes primary focus of personís activities; problems associated with drinking compound.

(Note: This is an example continuum. Remodel it to fit your own clientele or cirumstances)

The continuum is intended to lay out the progression of symptoms from abstinence to use, from use to misuse, from misuse to abuse and finally to dependence. It nicely supplements the elevator shaft described previously (step 4, figure 8), moving horizontally rather than vertically. It graphically and quickly illustrates the accumulation of negative consequences as the defeating relationship with alcohol both betrays and grows over time. When combined with the damage assessment (step 4, figure 7), a process I use with all my clients, the various stages of the denial system start to crumble.

To those clients who happily declare that they haven't reached the dependency level of the continuum, I respond, "Not yet" and point out that no one who gets that far on the continuum ever planned on it or wished for it. I further point out that those who do reach the dependency end of the scale were at one time or another exactly where the client is currently positioned. This moment of conversation in the therapy process becomes a perfect time to talk about the concept of "hitting bottom" and clarifying that bottom is simply that place on the elevator ride when a choice is finally made to 'get off' and another choice is made to 'start up'.

Denial Stages:

Stage I: There's *no* problem. If my drinking is a problem for you then that's your problem."
(No acceptance and no ownership)

Stage II: "There *was* a problem but it's now under control. I've cut back, only drink beer and only on the weekend."
(Historical problem)

Stage III: "I *have* a problem and I've quit drinking. But, I *don't* need any help and I'm definitely not going to AA."
(Minimizes seriousness and amount of work to be done)

Stage IV: "I *have* a problem, I've quit drinking and I need help. But not for long and I'll do it my way."
(Increased ownership and acceptance but forgets that their best thinking got them where they are now)

Stage V: "I *have* a problem, I need help and I'll do *whatever* it takes. Please help me."
(Complete ownership, acceptance and surrender)

In spite of the overwhelming damaging evidence of their relationship with alcohol, the decision to get off the downward elevator and begin the 12 steps upward is frequently conflictual. Some clients (Stage I) simply deny or minimize the reality of their floor on the elevator and walk away. Others (Stage II) wrestle and flirt with the age-old temptation to manipulate and control their drinking into a successful relationship. Still others (Stage V) mostly the minority, throw in the towel, surrender and open their hearts and minds as I prepare them and lead them to AA, further therapy, relapse prevention strategies and a continuing recovery program.

My heart goes out to those who deny their drinking problem and 'walk away'. As they leave, I know that I or another substance abuse therapist will eventually see them again when the predictable downward path of their elevator ride generates further grief and damage. When they do come back, sometimes months or years later, they're typically in greater pain and full of guilt and shame for not heeding the direction and encouragement given during our initial session(s). At this special moment, I always and tenderly tell them, "You got here as soon as you could! If you believe you're now ready, let's go to work and rediscover and recover your life."

But even then, because of the powerful physical and psychological draw of alcoholism, some clients will opt for yet another run at controlled drinking through willpower. My response is to once again dust off their previous damage assessment and then do a current one to illustrate the compounded suffering and the lower floor they now occupy on the elevator shaft. At this point, in whatever creative way I can, I attempt to teach them that there's no such word as "alcohol-wasm" and that their best thinking about drinking has gotten them where they now find themselves. I tell them that it's not their fault anymore than it's the fault of a diabetic for not being able to tolerate hot fudge sundaes. I also point out that if the diabetic continues to make the self-defeating choice of eating hot fudge sundaes, that choice and the guaranteed misery to follow......... "is their fault." This kind of 'teaching talk' in the therapy process is my way to direct and focus a psychic spotlight on their conscious mind and to raise the bottom on the elevator shaft. Depending upon the level of suffering and readiness, many times it works. When it doesn't, a guided controlled drinking experiment often becomes the next step in the consciousness raising experience.

Since many of my clients are below the legal drinking age, I don't encourage controlled drinking....particularly with those at the abuse and dependency level of the continuum. But when they refuse to surrender and instead insist upon a willpower approach at intake control, I use this denial to offer an invitation to participate in a personal experiment aimed at limiting the frequency and volume of their drinking. This invitation rapidly becomes a challenge and an opportunity to 'prove' that they can drink like average social drinkers on the other end of the continuum where they too used to be. The three parameters of the experiment are then framed by me.....not the client! They include: A. Defining a drink; B. Defining the consumption level and C., Defining the experiment time period. A drink is defined as a 12 oz. beer, 4 oz. glass of wine or a 1.5 ounce (measured) shot of liquor. Each of these contains approximately the same amount of alcohol. The consumption level is defined as follows: The client is entitled to no more than three drinks in a 24 hour period of time, no more than three times per week. I find that special emphasis is required to distinguish between 24 hours and days of the week. They're not the same! Failure to do so is guaranteed to prompt the "stacking" of drinks, i.e., three during the final hours of a Friday followed immediately by three more during the beginning hours of a Saturday for a total of six (or more) in 24 hours. Setting the experiment time period is extremely important because many abusive drinkers can successfully follow this 'recipe' for a week or even two. In fact, many completely stop drinking for short periods of time and then use the outcome as a way to deceive themselves into once again believing "there's no problem". The issue, of course, is staying with the 'recipe' or 'staying stopped'. For this reason, I set two months for the experiment time period and I tell each client that words like "success, failure, win, lose" are not to be connected with their results. The only thing that matters is "what are you learning about you and your relationship with alcohol?" I ask them to keep a log or journal, see me weekly during the experiment and simply and honestly report how it's going and what they're learning.

I'm pleased to report that over the years this controlled drinking experiment has been wonderfully instructional for many of my clients. While some (few) have been able to correct and reverse the continuum direction, most have found the experiment results otherwise and used the two month experience to open their conscious minds, surrender, get off the elevator and make the life-generating choice to begin the 12 step process toward rediscovery and recovery. At this powerful time of surrender, I have been repeatedly thankful for what I've been told is a 2000 year-old Japanese proverb which, in its three sentences, ever so nicely couples self-defeating behavior theory with alcohol addiction. It says:

First the person takes a drink.
Then the drink takes a drink.
Then the drink takes the person.

When problem drinkers are finally and seriously ready to get off the elevator, they're then capable of understanding the ancient wisdom of this proverb. They know that the first sentence is indeed a choice and, for them, a self-defeating choice. They know that the second sentence is not a choice but instead a consistently predictable bio-chemical involuntary reaction within their bodies. And, thanks to their work with the damage assessment (step 4), they know that the final sentence is the ultimate consequence of repeating the defeating choice made in the proverb's first sentence.

So, let me conclude this section of the book by noting that life presents us with many situations and conditions we didn't ask for and don't deserve. Conditions like multiple sclerosis, diabetes, alcoholism, etc. Nonetheless and fortunately, we have the gift of choice in how we respond to such conditions. We can take a two pound problem and turn it into two tons, thereby diminishing or destroying our lives as well as the lives of others around us. Or, we can use the same gift to accept our various conditions, deal with them and responsibly grow in spite of them. In the case of alcohol addiction, we have available to us the choices and techniques set forth in Part Three (figure 9) of this book.

It's important to keep in mind that substance abuse is obviously defeating but, in the context of this theory, may not be the primary self-defeating behavior. Alcohol and any other mood-altering substance could also be used as a technique to help implement a self-defeating behavior. It could equally be a result, a way to minimize or part of the disowning process of any number of self-defeating behaviors. Hence, the purpose and function of the substance abuse must be examined in light of the material presented in Part Two (how self-defeating behaviors are maintained and perpetuated).

FUTURE DIRECTIONS

The paths to a meaningful life and an indifferent existence
both lead uphill. Which will you choose?

This final section will address the present and possible future applications of the self-defeating behavior theory. We'd also like to take this opportunity to share some of the success stories we've received from individuals over the past years as they've embraced and applied the theory in a variety of settings.

Self-Help Application
LGB:
As Greg mentioned in the beginning of the book, the first edition, called "Goin' Home" was written with the intention that it supplement his classes and workshops. To his surprise, before long the book was being used as an independent self-help resource. Our hope is that this revised and expanded edition, when paired with effort and action, will become even more useful as a self-help and psychoeducational tool. To facilitate that hope, I urge anyone interested to find a partner or a small group of like-minded individuals to discuss the book and support each other's application and growth. I would also remind readers that our book is not intended to replace therapy or appropriate psychological services, but rather serve as a path for greater self-understanding, empowerment and personal growth. It encourages identifying and committing to life-generating choices.

For Mental Health Practitioners
Many counselors and psychologists in training have read the book and been trained in applying this model in their clinical work with clients. One strength of the theory is that it can be easily integrated into any theoretical orientation without major conflict or difficulty. Therapists often purchase extra copies of our book to offer to their clients. One such therapist shared a wonderful note of her success using the self-defeating theory with her clients:

> *"One of the many things I appreciate about your book is the elegance and simplicity with which the concept of self-defeating patterns is presented. My clients report feeling empowered, as if they are finally able to have some control back in their lives. It gives them something concrete to do, so they don't have to feel helpless or hopeless......For myself and my clients, this book is a guide through the landscape of our*

thinking and decision making processes. It gives us a map out of chaos and confusion, into a place of mastery and self-confidence."

For more complex and chronic psychopathology, this theory alone will not suffice. However, serious mental illness treated with traditional methods has been successfully augmented with the use of this theory. Cases of helpful application for those with obsessive compulsive disorders, phobias and other anxiety disorders have been frequently reported. The theory has also been used to help those who have obtained mental health sustain their well-being and not relapse back into major depression. It can help those with bi-polar disorder remain compliant with their medication and treatment protocol, a notorious challenge for these individuals. Some kinds of resolution require a combination of therapy, medication and long term treatment. Self-defeating behavior theory may offer one piece of the puzzle for treating these pervasive and complex psychopathologies.

Prevention/Psychoeducation
Individuals have suggested to us that an adaptation of the theory could effectively be used to help children and developing adolescents learn how to choose the life-generating path and perhaps prevent difficulties from developing in the first place. Certainly some of the more common self-defeating behaviors such as inferiority, shyness, negativity and perfectionism develop in childhood. We believe that children could learn to raise their emotional/psychological intelligence to such a degree that fewer self defeating behaviors would take root in their psychic gardens. It's a wonderfully hopeful thought.

For Couples
The relational defeating chapter lays the groundwork for couples who are walking the path 'home' together. The book can be read and applied together as partners. Couples therapists are adapting the theory and report finding it extremely useful helping couples (and families) to see the defeating patterns within their relationships, as well as their own patterns and contributions to the system as a whole.

Systems Work
Whether the system is a family wishing to function in a life generating way or looking at the constellation of individuals in a workplace setting, the systemic chapter offers suggestions for renovating and promoting growth within systems. We have brought workshops into numerous professional settings to successfully help employees, colleagues and co-workers gain a sense of systemic defeating behaviors and how to eliminate them.

Health Promotion/Health Behaviors

The self defeating behavior theory can be applied within numerous health settings. For example, patients with health conditions such as diabetes or heart disease would benefit from making long-standing life style changes. A non-compliant diabetic who then follows the steps of the theory will better understand and accept responsibility for making life generating choices in his/her diet and physical activity. Given that the major causes of death in developed countries are due to poor lifestyle choices, the impact of this theory could be tremendous. Presently, I teach the theory in many settings as a means of promoting healthy life style choices and the value of remaining committed to the choice through psychic gardening and ongoing maintenance of life generating health behaviors. Those involved in holistic health settings also find this theory easily adaptive for those who wish to balance mind, body and spirit.

Addictions

The previous chapter on substance abuse treatment addresses this application thoroughly and has been applied successfully in this area for a number of years. Many types of addictions have been broken through the use of the SDB theory, including smoking and the chewing of tobacco. Other people report ending long-standing gambling addictions thanks to the clarity of the theory and the subsequent help of support groups. These stories are encouraging.

Eating Issues

Another somewhat unexpected application comes from numerous individuals who share stories of recovering from eating disorders and compulsive eating. A therapist who attended a workshop many years ago has kept Greg informed of her progress with compulsive eating:

> "I thought you'd enjoy hearing that, 2 1/2 years later, my personal results remain solid. The compulsive eating 'beast' still lurks there in the background, waiting for me to forget how to do what I learned is necessary. I can't believe how comfortable a relationship I have finally found with food and with my physical self. I have gone on to use the SDB exercises with probably 150 clients so far, most often with very useful results. You helped me immeasurably, and in so doing, empowered me to go on to help many, many others far more effectively than I probably would have done otherwise."

Professional Coaching

The field of professional psychological coaching is predicted to be the next

105

major applied area in mental health promotion services. Coaching is very different from therapy in several important ways. First, coaching tends to be centered in the present and future as well as more action oriented. There is little emphasis on the past, especially childhood experiences. A coach works collaboratively with clients to create strategies for increasing life satisfaction and reaching goals. Part of this process includes getting rid of self-sabotaging or obstacles to growth and change. Eliminating self defeating behaviors and emphasizing life generating choices is an ideal tool in a professional coach's toolbox. I believe the future will bring increased public awareness of professional coaching services. Coaches will benefit from learning about the self defeating behavior theory as will their clients.

In Closing: An invitation

Were it not for the many stories that individuals have shared with us, there wouldn't be a place for the theory to soar and grow. This theory is alive and grows as we continue to learn from our clients, students and readers. We invite and encourage you to share your stories and responses to the book and your application of the ideas within these pages. What are you learning? What's working? What alterations would you recommend? Please email us or if you prefer, mail a 'good old fashioned' letter and help us light the path further as we share this journey going Home. You'll find our contact information on the final pages of the book. With gratitude, we look forward to hearing of your travels leading Home.

"In the beginning of love,
in the beginning of the day,
in the beginning of any work-
there is a moment when we understand
more perfectly than we understand again
until all is finished." - Yeats

CONCLUDING REMARKS

**"Goin' home, goin' home, I'm jes' goin' home;
It's not far, jes' close by, through an open door.
I'm jes' goin' home."**

GB:

Dr. Cudney's Theory of Eliminating Self-Defeating Behaviors has been responsible for finding the "open door" through which many individuals, couples and systems have been able to go home. Forever in my memory is the special example of a woman who enrolled in one of my workshops and sat miserably in the very back corner of the room without saying a word for the entire three-day experience. On the very last day of the workshop, she walked into the room with a giant, genuine smile and, before she could sit down I said, "You look radiant, what's that grin about?" Standing in front of her workshop colleagues she replied, "I feel radiant and alive because it's gone." "What's gone?" I asked. "My self-defeating behavior of fear of baking" she responded..... "it's gone!"

Although "fear of baking" was a new one on me, I could tell by her excitement that she had clearly rediscovered and recovered something powerful in her life. When I invited her to share her joy, she revealed the following story. As a child, she lived with her mother and grandmother who spent practically all of their time in the kitchen baking. Each time she tried to become a part of the baking experience and model after them, they would criticize and scold her with remarks like "Look at the mess you're making, what's wrong with you? How many times have I told you not to do that—can't you do anything right or are you just too dumb? Get out of here." These repeated doses of rejection produced immense pain and a deep sense of personal worthlessness. Baking became an emotionally dangerous proposition. Staying away from it brought relief.

At the time of the workshop, she was 37 years old and the mother of four school-age children. As an active homemaker and member of the neighborhood community, she regularly participated in coffee-klutches with other mothers during which one of the customs was to share homemade baked goods. In order to be a part of this sharing custom, she would disguise herself the day before the get-together and surreptitiously drive 40 miles to buy fresh baked goods from a bakery in another city and then drive 40 miles back praying all the while that nobody recognized her. When she returned home, she'd rewrap each of the items and attach a personalized custom-made label which she had ordered from a gourmet kitchen catalog to indicate that the items were baked in her own kitchen. As we continued listening to her astonishing story, she reported that she had carried on this scam for the past eleven years and that the damage assessment circle exercise in Step Four had finally dismantled her denial and brought her to her bottom. When she honestly acknowledged the cumulative toll of painful results from her behavior including fear, lies, worry, deceit, shame and money spent on each bakery road trip, it was time to get off the elevator. Especially, it was time to surrender a behavior which, for years, had gotten between her and her own self-respect.

When I asked why she was so happy that particular day she replied, "Because last night I did it, I did it, I did it. I made three loaves of whole wheat bread from scratch." Her enthusiastic description of her last night's accomplishment prompted an immediate and unsolicited question of doubt from another workshop member who obviously still trusted his own phony conclusion and mythical fears and was, therefore, desperately holding onto his self-defeating behavior. "How did it turn out?" he yelled suspiciously. "It was horrible," she replied, "and bless my husband's heart, he even ate some of that s...t!" Upon hearing her response, the man who had asked the question became visibly relieved. He appeared privately delighted over her failed bread-baking experience because he could now use it as encouragement to continue his own self-defeating cycle. When she saw his reaction she said, "I don't think you understand. The point is that last night I did it and, although it didn't turn out the way I'd hoped, I can't wait to get home tonight and try it again because I think I know where I made my mistakes. The important thing is that I didn't let my failed effort become a failed me. I don't have to do that anymore!"

The lesson from this story that's so worthy of acknowledging as Lori and I conclude this book is that change is a gradual process which takes place in phases over time. It requires effort and patience and an understanding that even when we practice life-generating behaviors, we will occasionally experience moments of distress, worry, disappointment and unhappiness. It's all part of the deal of accepting life on life's terms.

We wish you well on your journey home and, as a final contribution to your trip, leave you with another story. It's one my favorites. Like the music of "Goin' Home," it unlocks the heart and the path to peace. It was given to me at the end of a course by one of my graduate students who wished to remain anonymous and to whom I'll be forever grateful. As you read it, keep in mind the words of Carl Jung — "Learn your theories as well as you can but put them aside when you touch the miracle of the living soul." (1954)

Dear Greg:
I leave you with a story from my heart. I hope it will reveal my spiritual convictions in a way that rational sentences never quite capture.

My grandparents lived on a small 50 acre farm on the rolling hills of Michigan. I was always grandpa's favorite—something which was understood but not spoken. As a present, he gave me a calf to raise and care for with the long-range goal of showing at the county fair. I loved my calf and watched her grow into a beauty and eventually take second place at the county fair. After the fair, my grandfather said that the next step would be to take her to the auction which I knew all along was part of the plan. Prize winning cows fetch great prices at the auction and are often used for breeding purposes. I knew that other boys would also be at the auction with their prized animals. One gained a great deal of status in the eyes of his peers if their cow went for a good price.

Well, the day finally came to take my cow to the auction and, with great anticipation, I looked forward to see what kind of price my cow would fetch. At the check-in, all the cows were numbered and penned so that prospective buyers could inspect the animals to determine how much they would bid. I received a paddle with my cow's number which I was to hold up with pride as the bids came in. In my excitement, however, I failed to secure my cow properly in the pen and when a bull was brought by, she bolted, broke her neck and died.

My grandpa, being "old school," was very angry and said as punishment for my carelessness I would still be expected to walk into the "pit" and hold up my number. So, when the time came and my number was called, I walked into the pit, paddle in one hand, empty halter in the other and a sea of blank faces and deafening silence. The auctioneer began in the standard sing-song manner: "Going once!" My head hung down in shame. "Going twice!" Thank God this is almost over because I'm going to start crying; the painful lump in my throat is about to burst. "Going three times!" And then a strong, quiet voice rang out from the back of the crowd, "One hundred dollars." "Going once, twice..." "Two hundred dollars." "Going once, twice...." "Three hundred dollars!" "Going once, twice, three times, sold!" I didn't understand. All I knew was that my heart hurt less.

Not long after, I met the man who bought my dead cow and asked

109

him to explain why. I can still visualize the love in his eyes when he said, "Son, some investments can't be measured in dollars and cents or profits on returns. What's most essential in life cannot be seen with the human eye, one can only see rightly with the eyes of the heart."

Thank you Greg for a wonderful class. May God give your heart all the joy, peace, mercy and grace possible in this world.

AUTHORS' NOTES

When writing the first edition titled "Goin' Home", Greg remembers thinking it was going to be a lengthy book. It felt that way each time he cleared off the porch table, lit the wood stove, got out his yellow legal pad and felt tipped pen and continued writing. Midway through the second section, it started to look more like a "booklet". By the time he got to the third and final section, the word "pamphlet" was crossing his mind. With a smile, he recalls feeling fortunate that a fourth or fifth section wasn't added lest the whole thing would have run the risk of becoming a "handout" or "memo".

This revised edition with the slightly altered title of "Going Home" has more length and substance to it. Thanks to the insightful and fresh ideas from Lori, old and irrelevant stuff has been discarded and a much needed fourth section was added. Throughout the expansion and revision, we have attempted to retain the book's original spirit and intent to be helpful, manageable and pleasing. We hope that's been your experience and we thank you for reading "Going Home".

BIBLIOGRAPHY

Alcoholics Anonymous World Services, Inc., Box 459, Grand Central Station, New York, NY 10163

Csikszentmihalyi, M. (1990). Flow: The psychology of optimal experience. New York: Harper & Row.

Cudney, Milton R., and Robert E. Hardy. Self-Defeating Behaviors. New York: Harper Collins Publisher, 10 East 53rd St., New York, NY, 10022. 1991.

Gershon, D., & Straub, G.(1989). Empowerment: The art of creating your life as you want it. High point press.

Kinney, J.P. (2000). "The Cold Within", Liguorian, January edition.

Ram Dass (1992). The Listening Heart. Hanuman Foundation Tape Library. San Francisco, CA.

Seligman, M.E.P.(2002). Authentic Happiness. New York: Free Press.

Seligman, M.E.P., & Csikszentmihalyi, M.(2000). Positive psychology: An introduction. American Psychologist, 55(1), 5-14.

For more information about positive psychology and Authentic Happiness Coaching, please go to www.authentichappiness.org.

ABOUT THE AUTHORS

Gregory Boothroyd became involved as an experimenter and practitioner with the Self-Defeating Behavior Theory during its inception in the Counseling Center of Western Michigan University, Kalamazoo Michigan.

After narrating the film "Eliminating Self-Defeating Behaviors", he began to lead a number of workshops with students and faculty on Western's campus. The excitement generated through the success of these early workshops subsequently led to his own personal refinement of this therapeutic approach and further workshops at the state and national level.

Using this treatment model, he has trained counselors, social workers, psychologists, chemical dependency therapists, medical and court personnel across the nation and, with warmth and engaging humor, is a frequent keynote presenter and trainer at national conventions on the inception, maintenance and elimination of self-defeating behaviors.

Dr. Boothroyd earned his Bachelor's and Master's degrees at Western Michigan University, and his Ph.D. from The University of Michigan. He is a certified addictions counselor, licensed professional counselor, and distinguished faculty member of the Michigan Judicial Institute in the area of substance abuse assessment and treatment. He holds the rank of Professor Emeritus of Counseling at Western Michigan University where he also served as University Ombudsman and Director of University Substance Abuse Services.

Dr. Lori G. Boothroyd holds a Ph.D. in Counseling Psychology from Michigan State University. She also has a masters degree and a specialty graduate certificate in Holistic Health Care from Western Michigan University. Lori was a music major and aspiring trumpet player as an undergraduate student at The University of Michigan, when she also discovered a passion for helping herself and others attain life balance and satisfaction.

Lori is a doctoral limited licensed psychologist and a committed coach whose goal is to listen deeply to her clients, ask powerful questions and co-create strategies for reaching client goals. She trains through the Mentorcoach program, a highly respected training program for learning powerful coaching methods. She is dedicated to ongoing training of advanced clinical techniques and expanding her practice. She is a graduate of the Authentic Happiness Coaching training program, directed by Dr. Martin Seligman and grounded in the principles of positive psychology and the goal of increasing the "tonnage" of happiness in the world.

Currently a Visiting Professor for Western Michigan University's Holistic Health Care program, Lori was previously a Professor of Psychology at Kalamazoo College, a liberal arts college in Kalamazoo, Michigan. Most recently, she opened an independent private practice (Life Expansion Psychological Services) and offers psychotherapy and coaching services.

To learn more about our workshops and services, purchase additional copies of "Going Home", or contact us to share your stories please visit our website: www.drboothroyd.com. To send us email: lori.boothroyd@yahoo.com and gregoryboothroyd@yahoo.com. To mail an old fashioned letter or mail a book order:

Honu Publications

P.O. Box 601
Traverse City, MI 49685
ph: 231-228-2330, fax: 231-228-2334

Thank you!
Gregory and Lori Gray Boothroyd

www.drboothroyd.com
www.honupublications.com
www.lifeexpansion.com

Order Form

"Going Home: A positive emotional guide to promote life generating behavior"
By: Drs. Gregory and Lori Boothroyd
Honu Publications

Please print:

Name: _____

Address: _____

City: _____ State: _____ Zip: _____

Phone Number: _____ Email address: _____

Please send form with a check for $16.95 (includes shipping and handling) for each copy requested to:
Honu Publications
P.O. Box 601
Traverse City, MI 49685

Questions? Call 231-228-2330. Thank you!